SUFFER THE LITTLE CHILDREN

SUFFER THE LITTLE CHILDREN

*Christians, Abortion, and
Civil Disobedience*

Mark Belz, M.Div., J.D.

CROSSWAY BOOKS • WESTCHESTER, ILLINOIS
A DIVISION OF GOOD NEWS PUBLISHERS

To Linda, Aaron, and Jane
for their loving support

TABLE OF

CONTENTS

ACKNOWLEDGMENTS

*G*od used my family and friends to help me write this book. My brothers Joel and Tim gave up chunks of their time to aid the endeavor, and many other family members gave practical advice and encouragement. Several clergymen have helped: Lin Crowe, whose exposition of Scripture contributed to Chapter Four; David Jones, who has discussed many of the issues in this book with me, and who helped me formalize some of the ideas by letting me teach his seminary ethics class; Ron Lutjens, David Winecoff, and George Knight shared their insights and encouraged me to continue. There are others to thank. Sam Lee's months of imprisonment for his attempts to defend unborn children awakened my conscience; his friendship and kindly counsel have been a constant inspiration. Ann O'Brien and the scores of other St. Louis regulars have given our law firm the high privilege of representing them in their unflagging efforts to protect the unborn. My associates Lynn Beckemeier, Tim Belz, Terry Jones, John Decker, and Augie Beckemeier gave me latitude in working hours to finish the manuscript. Herb Ward read the manuscript carefully and gave me continuing encouragement. Doug Skrainka and Mark Jones did research in the early stages of the project. And most of all I want to thank Marvin Olasky, who works too hard and stays up too late, but who has been a great help and a good friend to this inexperienced writer.

PREFACE

On July 19, 1988, hundreds of Christians assembled in Atlanta to engage in a "rescue" of unborn children about to be destroyed by abortion. Their effort, led by pro-life activist Randall Terry, was dubbed Operation Rescue.

Those who participated knew at the outset that their intervention at the doors of Atlanta's abortion clinics would have some nasty consequences. They expected many of their number to be arrested and jailed, and they were not disappointed. Long before July 19, most of them had already decided that they were willing to be arrested for this cause—convinced that in their resistance to abortion, an illegal act may be right and proper.

The Atlanta protesters made the national news on that day, the first day of the Democratic National Convention. They made the news on every successive day that week, as more and more were arrested and jailed. The operation continued into the next week, and the week after that, and the week after that. By mid-August, the number arrested exceeded seven hundred. Pastors and laypeople alike continued to sit down in front of the doors of the abortion clinics in the Atlanta area, blocking entry to women seeking abortions, and refusing to move when asked.

Though most protesters were charged with minor violations such as trespass, authorities would not release them until they gave their names and addresses, something most of them were unwilling to do. It was through anonymity, after all, that they intended to show solidarity with the unborn child, who, like them, suffers because he is unnamed and without identification.

As a result of refusing to be identified, hundreds of protesters remained in jail for months. The last batch of those arrested in the summer who had refused to give their names was finally released—still anonymous prisoners—in the first week of December 1988. Some of the pastors (who could be identified) were considered by the authorities to be ringleaders and were therefore charged with an additional, more serious crime under Georgia law: conspiring to commit a misdemeanor. The conspiracy charge is a felony.

The Atlanta protest was just part of a growing movement in the United States in which Christians engage in nonviolent civil disobedience in resistance to abortion. Ever since the 1973 *Roe v. Wade* decision by the United States Supreme Court legalized abortion nationwide, resistance to the new law has been evident. Civil disobedience has always been part of that resistance, but not to the extent that it is now.

Apparently the significance of that Supreme Court decision did not immediately register with many American evangelicals. Many Protestant believers opposed the 1973 decision, but thought that it was just another all-too-predictable product of an always-too-liberal Supreme Court. There was almost a collective shoulder shrug: what else is new?

Besides, the "pro-life movement" was widely perceived as Roman Catholic. Abortion was sometimes vaguely seen as a companion to birth control[1]—and everyone knew that it was the Catholic Church which was officially opposed to birth control. By tossing abortion and birth control into the same mental basket, many evangelicals found it fairly easy to live with abortion-on-demand—even though they were theoretically opposed to it.

It is true that the early bands of "rescuers" were mostly Catholics. John Cavanaugh O'Keefe is credited with organizing the first sit-in at an abortion clinic in Rockville, Maryland, in 1975, when he and six women entered the clinic offices uninvited and attempted to dissuade patients seeking abortions. Joan Andrews was another early activist. This single Catholic woman committed her life to fighting abortion and began her open, peaceful, but illegal resistance at the doors of abortion clinics almost as soon as the 1973 decision was handed down. She was most recently released from jail in late 1988, after serving about half of a five-year sentence. She had attempted to remove an electrical cord from a suction machine used to perform abortions at a Florida clinic.

And so since 1973 the stream of civilly disobedient Christians (the pro-life movement has always been primarily made up of professing Christians) has continued with sometimes more, sometimes less national visibility. Until the mid-1980s, however, the number of people arrested was small. Somehow, from about 1984 on, more Christians became involved in direct resistance to abortion. Perhaps more people became aware of the facts of the abortion procedure, or saw photographs of aborted babies, or discovered the magnitude of the numbers of lives lost through abortion. (One-third of America's preborn infants are now aborted.) Some began to conclude that fifteen years of political and legal strategizing had failed, and that it was time to take a more direct approach.

Whatever the reason, more and more Christians perceived that they had not given the abortion issue high enough priority in their lives. It was an issue that could not remain in the shadows forever. Unless action was taken, abortion-on-demand was apparently here to stay, having been given the status of a right guaranteed by the law. The killing of unborn children was now an activity protected by the courts and policemen of America. Slowly but surely the moral concern which had always been present was developing into a sense of moral outrage.

More Protestants (almost entirely from evangelical churches) became engaged in the battle, even participating in illegal nonviolent resistance at the door of the clinic. The *Wall Street Journal* estimated that by the end of 1988 the nonviolent direct action movement, which once had been 90 percent Catholic, was now 60 percent Protestant.[2]

In the Spring of 1988 more than sixteen hundred arrests were made in New York during a single week. Large sit-ins occurred in Philadelphia, Cincinnati, and St. Louis. In many other cities across the United States, more and more people who identified themselves as Christians were placing themselves in front of doors, on sidewalks, and in corridors at America's abortion clinics, determined to do what they could do to halt the killing of the unborn. Although such illegal efforts vary somewhat from time to time and place to place, Operation Rescue's Randall Terry has offered this simple descriptive definition of the kind of civil disobedience which was dominant in 1988, and which is the kind discussed in this book:

A rescue mission happens when one or two, or a group of twenty or a hundred or five hundred or more people go to an abortion clinic and either walk inside to the waiting room, offering an alternative to the mothers, or sit around the door of the abortion clinic before it opens to prevent the slaughter of innocent lives.[3]

Many of those involved in such rescues would argue that such acts are not fairly categorized as "civil disobedience," because the primary purpose of the act is not to violate an immoral law. It is true that Gandhi and Martin Luther King, Jr. usually employed the term to refer to the intentional violation of what they considered to be oppressive or immoral laws. Nevertheless, Operation Rescue's activity is "civil disobedience" in the broad definition of the term, because it involves the intentional violation of the law in an effort to serve a claimed higher purpose or higher law. It is this broader definition of the term that is used in this book.

These acts of civil disobedience have sharply divided the pro-life movement, particularly its evangelical component. Evangelical Christians who object to abortion are, for the most part, conservatives both in theology and politics. But to many, conservative Christianity and civil disobedience of any kind seem to be mutually exclusive terms, or at least strange bedfellows. Many of those who are now willing to go to jail to resist abortion can remember their own criticism of student anti-war demonstrators and even civil rights activists in the 1960s. These conservatives are likely to remember their own former disgust with those who would violate the law in order to work a change in the law, but ironically find themselves in a similar position now. Somehow they have been brought to the point where they believe abortion is so bad they are willing to violate the law in their resistance to it.

Those in the "mainstream," whose chief spokesman probably has been John Willke, head of the NRLC (National Right to Life Committee), are convinced that any illegal activity will have only a detrimental effect on the pro-life movement. Dr. Willke believes strongly that persistently addressing the issue through the legislatures and the courts will ultimately win the day. He feels that if pro-lifers are willing to disobey the law now, it only undermines the respect for the law that they would demand of others once the laws regarding abortion are changed. On the other hand, Operation Rescue's leaders believe that the halls of abortion clinics[4] should be filled with people directly confronting the killing.

But for participants in Operation Rescue, the issues are not altogether matters of tactics or strategy. Few of those who block doors at the abortion clinic are following a master plan for changing the law. Neither is it fair to say that they are acting heedlessly, out of sheer anger or frustration. Most of them would claim to be doing what they are doing simply as a matter of conscience. They believe that abortion is equivalent to murder, at least in its consequences for the unborn child. They believe that as a matter of conscience they must continue to write letters to the editor, sign petitions, and vote for pro-life candidates; but their consciences tell them that where possible they must do something more direct as well. And while their acts of conscience are not always strategic, they have an underlying confidence that being true to conscience in this matter will ultimately result in restored legal protection for the unborn, and that somehow a failure to act in accordance with conscience will corrode and, in the end, dissolve the entire pro-life effort.

It is not surprising that the greater Christian community is divided on the issue. Evangelical American Christianity during the last sixteen years has increasingly become identified with political conservatism. Political conservatives come in many shapes and sizes, but two prominent characteristics that mark them out in the present era are "pro-life" and "law-and-order." Evangelicals want both respect for life and respect for authority. At the door of the abortion clinic, these values collide.

It is this collision of values that this book seeks to address. In doing so, it needs to be said clearly at the outset that the battle against abortion is being waged—as it should be waged—on a multitude of important fronts. It is true that the primary scope of discussion in this book will be the propriety of the Christian's disobedience to the civil law in the abortion controversy. But the work being done in establishing adoption agencies, crisis pregnancy centers, and telephone hot lines—in political lobbying, publication and distribution of literature, education, sidewalk counseling, and all the rest—are of crucial importance in the battle for the unborn.

Where distinctions are drawn in this book between one sphere of activity and another—between that which is legal and that which is not—it is probable that the arguments will be viewed by some as a "putdown" of one group or the other, no matter how many disclaimers are made by the author. But in fact, all efforts in the battle against abortion that come from a sincere heart guided by the Word of God are worthy and significant. There are no second-class soldiers in this war.

ONE

THE WEIGHT OF
THE ABORTION ISSUE

*M*illions of contemporary Americans consider themselves "pro-life." Most of us who own that label mean to say we stand in opposition to abortion and to the current state of the law in our country. We reject the United States Supreme Court's 1973 decision of *Roe v. Wade*,[1] which radically changed existing law by ruling that every pregnant woman in the United States has a constitutional right to terminate the life of her unborn child.

We "pro-lifers"—as a matter of top national priority—want to see the Supreme Court reverse that decision, or we want to see the law changed in some other way. At the time of this writing, more than twenty-three million abortions have been carried out under *Roe v. Wade*, and we want it all to come to an end. We want to see unborn children in America again receive the protection of the law. We who are Christians also believe in a God of judgment, and we have a proper fear for the future of our country. We want to see America turned back to righteousness generally and in this particular matter before it is too late.

But why are we so singularly opposed to abortion in the first place? We say that abortion is morally wrong, but we do not believe that it is the only moral evil in our country. We see unjustified divorces, increasing levels of pornography, and perhaps even public lotteries (to name just a few) as moral wrongs too—all sanctioned by the laws of this country. For most of us, however, abortion seems to be in a completely different category. It is in a class by itself. It seems to loom over the multitude of other concerns as the principal moral issue of the day. Why?

We oppose abortion because we believe that abortion is the destruction of human life. But it is not just abortion in general and human life in general. We believe that each abortion is the taking of the life of an individual human being. The Bible teaches that every human being is created in the image of God, and the Sixth Commandment prohibits killing those created in God's image. If abortion is the intentional, unjustified destruction of another human being, then abortion is a clear violation of that commandment. A characteristic evangelical position statement on the nature of abortion has been set out by the Presbyterian Church in America:

> We cannot stress too strongly our authority in this matter. God in His Word speaks of the unborn child as a person and treats him as such, and so must we. The Bible teaches the sanctity of life, and so must we. The Bible, especially in the Sixth Commandment, gives concrete protection to that life which bears the image of God. We must uphold that commandment. . . . The Church as the repository of God's revelation must speak from that authority and must do so without compromise or equivocation.[2]

We need to recognize that when we say an abortion is the unjustified taking of a human life—a transgression of the Sixth Commandment—we have said more than we might like to admit. For the act of abortion under *Roe v. Wade* is always an intentional act. Presumably, an abortion contemplated by the *Roe v. Wade* Court must be carefully considered, planned, and carried out. And it always involves at least two people[3] (the woman and her doctor, at a minimum) who agree on carrying it out.[4] Thus, the act of abortion is by its very nature a premeditated act. We are driven to conclude that abortion is by definition the intentional, premeditated taking of a human life.

Is it hyperbole, then, to argue (as the pro-life picketers' signs proclaim) that abortion is murder? The Model Penal Code, which serves as a pattern for most states' criminal laws, defines first-degree murder as purposely or knowingly causing the death of another person.[5] Many would object that abortion does not, strictly speaking, fit this definition, because of the word "knowingly." It is argued that the woman who asks for an abortion does not believe that she really is killing her baby; she believes that abortion is "removing tissue" or "terminating her pregnancy," but she really does not understand that the unborn fetus is a human being, and thus we could not justly say that she "knowingly causes the death of another person" in the act of abortion.

It goes without saying that it is impossible to judge the particular knowledge or understanding of every woman who chooses to abort her child. Approximately four thousand abortions are performed in the United States each day of the week. There are hundreds of doctors involved and four thousand different mothers. Each case is unique; there are obviously wide variations in the perceptions and understanding of the many women involved. In many of these cases, fifteen- and sixteen-year-olds (or younger) are the ones making the decision, and these young women are likely to be scared and confused about what is really going on. It is probable that few of them are fully informed, or fully aware, of what is taking place. It may be that they genuinely believe that the abortion is just a medical procedure that "terminates a pregnancy," without having any real appreciation of the biological reality of fetal development, or of the nature of the unborn child in the womb. Such a person is really a victim herself, along with her child, even though she is a participant in the decision to abort. It might be unreasonable, and unsympathetic, to hold such a person to a standard of "murder." She may lack the requisite intent, simply because she is ignorant of what is going on.

Nevertheless, while we must be careful not to impose an unjust judgment upon mothers who have chosen abortion, neither the women who abort nor the greater communities of church and society will benefit from refusing to face facts. Further, in the long run none of us will be damaged by facing facts. To the extent that a woman understands that she is carrying a preborn infant, and still chooses to have that infant destroyed, at least to that extent it must be said that she has violated the Sixth Commandment. If we wince as we come to that rather harsh conclusion, it is probable that we grossly underestimate two things: the radical nature of our sinful condition (the Bible teaches that we are all murderers by nature), and the radical nature of God's grace in dealing with our sin. Most of us wince because we have friends who have had abortions, and we do not want them to think that we accuse them of murder. But it is not by our authority that we make moral judgments in the first place. Thus we have no right to withdraw God's moral standard when it becomes particularly uncomfortable in a given situation. We must rather make the application of the moral Law with humility and compassion, recognizing fully our own weaknesses and susceptibility to doing that which God has forbidden.

The woman is not the only participant in a legal abortion. There is always a doctor. Unlike the woman, he can hardly plead confusion or ignorance. He is a licensed practitioner in the "healing arts," and must be held to the very highest standard of knowledge and care regarding the biological facts of prenatal life. He knows, or should be expected to know, that he is destroying a human life when he performs the abortion. But some still will object that regardless of what the doctor may objectively be doing in the abortion procedure, he could not be held morally responsible for murder because he has (whether mistakenly or not) adopted the position that the unborn child is not a human being; that when he performs an abortion, he is simply removing "fetal tissue." Such doctors hold a different view: they do not believe that the unborn child is a person. Thus, the argument goes, they lack the requisite intent for murder because of their view.

But is a doctor's subjective opinion regarding the humanity of the unborn when he performs an abortion really and ultimately the underlying issue? Do we grant such latitude to the Nazi doctor who killed Jews, simply because he held the view that Jews were less than human? Do we carve out an exception for the pre-Civil War slave owner who killed his slave because he had adopted the view that Negroes were not persons in the full sense of the word?

It is not as though the Nazi doctors and the slave owners were without official sanction. Hitler's Fascist government approved and ordered the slaughter of the Jews. There were reasoned court decisions by judges in the Third Reich to back up the decisions made by the doctors. And the United States Supreme Court ruled, in the *Dred Scott* decision,[6] that under the Constitution Negroes who had been slaves were not citizens but chattels—the personal property of the slave owner—and thus were not able to file a lawsuit in American courts, nor otherwise worthy of constitutional protection. As the years rolled on, both the 1857 United States Supreme Court and the Third Reich were proven to be tragically wrong. History found both to have violated unchangeable, universal moral Law. Courts and individuals along the way who held "views" that allowed them to break that higher law were not later excused—even by other men— simply because they claimed to have been mistaken.

Furthermore, if it is argued that one who aborts an unborn child lacks the requisite intent to murder a human being, because that individual does not believe the unborn child to be a person but perhaps only "tissue" or the like, we need to look again at the language in the *Roe v. Wade* decision. Justice Blackmun, who wrote the opinion adopted by the majority of the Court, outlined what were judged to be some of the principal, legitimate reasons on which a woman and her physician could base a decision to have an abortion:

> Maternity, or additional offspring, may force upon the woman a distressful life and future. Psychological harm may be imminent. Mental and physical health may be taxed by child care. There is also the distress, for all concerned, associated with the unwanted child, and there is the problem of bringing a child into a family already unable, psychologically and otherwise, to care for it. In other cases, as in this one, the additional difficulties and continuing stigma of unwed motherhood may be involved. All these factors the woman and her responsible physician necessarily will consider in consultation.[7]

Notice the common characteristic of each of these reasons. Every one of the considerations has to do with, or assumes, the personhood—the humanity—of the one who is to be destroyed. What—or who—is the object of an abortion? Tissue presents no threat. Tissue does not force upon the woman a distressful life and future. Tissue does not require a baby-sitter, nor does it present someone with the stigma of unwed motherhood. It does not require food, clothing, discipline, or tuition. There is only one reason for the consideration of an abortion, and that is precisely that a person—already existent—is involved, a person who, unless he is destroyed, threatens to burden both parent and society with these expenses, cares, and difficulties. The *Roe v. Wade* Court obviously understood what really goes into the abortion decision—that what is being destroyed is a human being, with the demands and burdens that only a human being can place on the child's mother and on the rest of society.

Before we go further, we need to recognize that it is precisely because abortion is the killing of another human being that we believe abortion is wrong. It could not be for a lesser reason. If abortion were really just the removal of tissue, or if it were nothing more than another method of birth control, or if it were anything short of the taking of a human life, would we have such radical concern? If abortion is wrong at all, it must be—and indeed is—because it destroys people.

"Pro-choice" advocates unwittingly make this point. Former Chief Justice of the United States Supreme Court Warren Burger, who voted with the majority in *Roe v. Wade*, has in a more recent abortion case expressed great concern about the ease with which women can obtain abortions, claiming that he never intended by the *Roe* decision to open the door to "abortion on demand."[8] The head of the largest abortion clinic in the St. Louis area has publicly proclaimed that it is important for everyone to work together to reduce the need for abortions (rather than spending time and effort protesting them). Echoing this theme, the *St. Louis Post-Dispatch*, a pronounced advocate of abortion "rights," published an editorial in June 1988 entitled, "Abortion Should Be a Last Resort," which set forth "shocking" statistics and an appeal:

> Researchers for the Alan Guttmacher Institute, an organization deal-ing in population issues, found that countries where a wide variety of contraceptives is available and easy to obtain have fewer unplanned pregnancies and fewer abortions than countries where the selection is limited and less accessible. The United States falls into the latter cat-egory. In 1983, the institute said, 51.2 percent of U.S. pregnancies were unplanned. In Great Britain, 31.8 percent were unplanned; in the Netherlands 17 percent. In contraceptive use, the United States ranked with Portugal and Spain. Based on current abortion rates in the United States, the researchers projected that among every 100 women there eventually will be 76 induced abortions—a shocking figure.... The lesson here is twofold. First, contraceptives must be more readily available and their use encouraged through educational programs.

Second, attitudes must be changed so that abortion becomes a last resort, not a routine form of birth control.[9]

Why so? Why is Justice Burger, thirteen years after he voted with the majority in *Roe v. Wade*, so concerned about abortion "on demand"? Why does the statistic showing that there will be seventy-six induced abortions per every one hundred American women earn the "shocking" tag? Why should abortion become a last resort if it is nothing more than the removal of tissue? Why should everyone be working together to reduce the need for abortions? If abortion is not killing, then there should be no concern about its availability "on demand." It would be absurd to all work together to reduce the need for the surgical removal of tissue. Are the editors of the *Post-Dispatch* equally shocked at the number of men who shave every morning, or at the number of Americans who trim their fingernails?

There is only one possible cause for this sense of wrongness, and that is that an abortion is the destruction of a human life. Even the abortionist recognizes the fact that a life—not just tissue—is taken in an abortion.

It is at this point that I may be tempted to back away from the issue a little. Yes, I say, abortion is the unjustified, premeditated taking of a human life. Yes, I admit, when the doctor performs an abortion, his act is equivalent to murder. But somehow I am willing to treat his killing of a fetus—an unborn child—differently from the killing of a born child or an adult. (Could it be that I am beginning to sense some of the radical ethical and moral implications that might result if I treat the unborn child as a person?)

But if I reflect for a few moments, it becomes clear that the only way in which I can permit myself to draw a difference between the born and the unborn is to value the life of one differently from the life of the other. It would mean that I would have to treat one as a person, in the full sense of the word, and one as something or someone less than a person. Then (whether I like it or not) I would be in basic agreement with the *Roe v. Wade* Court when the majority held that "the word 'person' . . . does not include the unborn."[10] Either the unborn is a person holding, with the rest of us, those minimum rights identified in the Declaration of Independence—life, liberty, and the pursuit of happiness—or he has no protectable rights at all. We discover that this is an either-or proposition. There is no room for luxuriating in differing shades of definition.

It is quite literally a life-and-death question. Either the unborn child is a person, and must be treated like a person, or he is no person at all, and should be treated like so much gristle—like a broken fingernail.

With that in mind, consider once again the definition of murder: purposely or knowingly, without justification, causing the death of another human being. If language has meaning, abortion is murder. But *Roe v. Wade* has made it legal.

We must face reality in America today. An abortion is a murder; abortion is legal; therefore, murder is legal. The entire machinery of the system of jurisprudence in America, since January 22, 1973, has been engaged to promote, protect, and preserve the carrying out of this right to kill. As of this writing, more than twenty-three million murders have been carried out, and one-third of all unborn American children are killed before they see the light of day. We are witnessing continuous, legal mass slaughter. We must face these facts.

This slaughter is particularly egregious for five reasons:

First, because *its victims are innocent by any human standard of justice.* The unborn child has committed no act worthy of the death penalty. People argue about the morality of the imposition of a death sentence on one convicted of a capital offense, but few would debate that the convict is at least worthy of severe punishment for what he has done. But by definition the unborn child has done nothing worthy of human punishment, let alone the imposition of the death sentence. His destruction is based wholly on the motives, perceived needs, feelings, and convenience of others. He is passive. If he is considered by others to be "in the way" and a burden, his life is taken, even though he is entirely without fault in the matter.

Second, because *its victims are helpless.* The Jewish Holocaust was unthinkably vile; the unarmed Jewish civilians were herded into boxcars and taken to death camps. It is always more outrageous to see unarmed civilians executed than to see even friendly armed military men shot and killed, because the soldier is at least able to attempt to mount a defense. The tiny unborn child is in no way able to defend himself or escape. He cannot run, he cannot beg, he cannot fight for his life. He is wholly at the mercy of others who can do all of those things. He is utterly vulnerable and dependent.

Third, because *the order to kill comes from the victim's mother.* In a *Roe v. Wade* abortion, the mother's decision to take her baby's life is always necessary before the life is taken. Unlike the Holocaust, and unlike similar atrocities in world history, in abortion the decision to kill comes from the one person from whom we would otherwise expect the greatest concern, the most help, the most intense desire to protect, preserve, and nurture. In an abortion the greatest natural bond of affection in our race is resisted, defied, shattered. A mother—even though she may be unaware of the brutality of the act—decides to have her child's life ended, and thus she participates in the killing.

Fourth, because *abortion is always a reasoned, intentional, calculated, conspiratorial act.* The *Roe v. Wade* Court listed the factors which a mother might consider in making her decision and then concluded: "All these factors the woman and her responsible physician necessarily will consider in consultation."[11] Presumably (or so we are assured by abortion clinics), the decision to abort is not made lightly. The mother and abortionist supposedly think it over carefully before they carry it out.[12] Whatever their reasoning process is, they almost always decide against the child, against his life and future. And thus they plan together—they conspire—to kill the child.

Fifth, because *the abortionist is paid for the killing.* A mother must hire a doctor to take the life of her unborn baby. *Roe v. Wade* and later cases make it clear that the mother must always obtain the considered advice and services of a doctor. In any system of jurisprudence, it is an undeniable perversion of justice to reward an arbiter or judge financially if he decides in such and such a way. But the chief adviser, the "judge," in the abortion decision is paid if he kills the baby; conversely, his annual gross income dips every time he says no. The baby has no money with which to outbid his mother and her doctor. As the mother who is not so sure she wants to be burdened with the responsibility of childrearing seeks advice from the abortionist-doctor, her only adviser, the deck is cruelly stacked against her child. The child awaits a verdict from a "judge" who will be paid off only if he decides against him. He cannot compete. The kid does not stand a chance.

This is not a new phenomenon in the annals of injustice and dehumanization. The profit motive has often played a significant role in the advancement of injustice. The Fugitive Slave Law of 1850, which imposed fines, penalties, and imprisonment on any citizen aiding the escape of a Negro slave, provided that the U.S. commissioner would be paid ten dollars if he found in favor of the slave owner, but only five if he found in favor of the slave.[13] Amazingly, the language of the federal statute tied the differentiation in the commissioner's pay to his evaluation of the evidence:

> . . . and in all cases where the proceedings are before a commissioner, he shall be entitled to a fee of ten dollars in full for his services in each case, upon the delivery of the said certificate to the claimant, his or her agent or attorney; or a fee of five dollars in cases where the proof shall not, in the opinion of such commissioner, warrant such certificate and delivery. . . .[14]

Of course, to the reader who remains unconvinced that the unborn child is a person, these arguments beg the question. But this book is not directed to those holding such a view. Its primary purpose is not to prove that the unborn child is a person, nor to prove that abortion is murder, because most of its audience will likely already hold that opinion. Still, the unconvinced reader is urged to reexamine the evidence. The medical evidence is increasingly convincing in confirming that the unborn child is a human being (but, of course, medical science does not even really help too much in making that kind of determination about adults). Photographic evidence is perhaps the most objective, realistic, and convincing. It is relatively painless for us to discuss this issue dispassionately in theory only, attempting to keep a safe distance from the baby's body. A photograph normally does not misrepresent the facts, and it is capable of piercing that protective veil. We see the photograph of the aborted baby, and we know instinctively that this bloody, broken body is one of us. He is no longer out of sight, out of mind. There is no doubt. Look at the child. He has a nose, eyes, ears, fingers, legs, and toes. He is our little brother.

Children have an uncanny way of seeing through rhetoric; it was a child who saw that the emperor had no clothes. In May 1984 an abortion center in Milwaukee named Bread and Roses mistakenly allowed about twenty-five bodies of preborn children from a day or so of work to be placed in a garbage dumpster. The dumpster was in back of the abortion clinic, near a vacant lot frequented by five- and six-year-old children. The children found the remains of the aborted preborns and began to play with them. Onlookers called the police. When the police arrived at the scene, they asked the children what they were doing. The children answered that they had been playing with "the little people."[15]

On this matter of identifying a being as human, the Supreme Court, philosophers, doctors, and theologians have, through convoluted reasoning and argumentation, made a rather simple matter very complex. When I drive down a highway, I instinctively differentiate, say, dogs and humans. When a dog runs across the path, I instantly recognize that being as a dog; when a child darts out from behind a parked car, I recognize that being as a person. Recognition is not the only way, but it is the primary way in which we identify beings as "persons" every day of our lives. We see someone—we identify him (without philosophizing on the matter) as one of "us." We do not demand any other identification whatsoever.

It is thus not a matter of my imputation of humanity to that person that makes him so; it is rather a matter of my recognition of him as a fellow-member of my race. Like Adam, my immediate observation upon viewing another person is, "This is now bone of my bones and flesh of my flesh."[16]

We do not define abortion as murder in this book in order to build a case against mothers and doctors who abort. The focus must be trained on the child. It is true that insofar as his life is concerned, it matters little if he is murdered or if he dies in an automobile accident. Either way he winds up dead. But it is important to call a spade a spade. If we recognize the unborn child as a human being, and if his life is purposely or knowingly taken, we need to call the act "murder" for our benefit, if for no other purpose. We must gain accurate perspective if we are to understand and feel the weight of the issue, so that we can respond adequately.

But once the weight of the issue is felt, there remains a different, and maybe a more frightening, challenge. It is a challenge for every one of us who claims to recognize the humanness of the unborn child: are we acting in a way that is consistent with what we say we believe?

THE DEMAND FOR MORAL INTEGRITY

A few years ago I heard an interview on my car radio between a local reporter and a nationally known pro-choice advocate. When the reporter asked the woman whether or not she believed the abortion procedure was really the destruction of another human life, she said, "Of course we do not believe that abortion is murder. But we don't believe that the pro-life people really think so either. If they do, they certainly don't act like it."

I switched the radio off in anger. As the pro-choicers bask in the "rights" granted them by the United States Supreme Court in 1973, and blithely go around advocating the propriety of this new-found freedom, one of their spokeswomen takes time off to fire a shot over her shoulder at us. She is hardly the one to challenge our integrity, I fumed. We'll take criticism from our friends, but not from her.

But as I drove along and considered more calmly what she had said, I remembered what another woman had taught me many years before. Marian Draper, my fifth grade teacher, used to post an old saying on the bulletin board of our one-room schoolhouse in Iowa. It said:

YOUR ACTIONS ARE SPEAKING SO LOUDLY THAT I CANNOT
HEAR WHAT YOU ARE SAYING.

Sadly, this proverb accurately assesses the voice of much of the Christian community today on abortion. And to that extent, the pro-choice spokeswoman had stated the truth, never mind her motives. Does the world really hear what we are saying about abortion? Are our political leaders, judges, and legislators really hearing the message we want them to hear? Is there reason for them to believe it? Or are our actions—or lack of actions—speaking so loudly no one can hear what we are saying?

There is probably no higher compliment to pay another person than to say that he has integrity. A man who has integrity means what he says. His words are not empty; his actions match his speech. The word *integrity* actually means "wholeness," "completeness," or "oneness." That is, the man as a speaker and the man as a doer is consistent: he is whole, complete, one.

By definition, it is not possible to possess or display integrity simply by talking about it. No matter how convincing my elaborate promises to my wife that I will remember to take out the garbage before I leave for the office in the morning, the bags of garbage on the curb—and only the bags of garbage on the curb—ultimately will convince her. My integrity is shown only in action consistent with my words; it can never be determined from my words alone. If I leave the trash in the basement day after day, my words mean less and less and communicate, at best, a bare intention.

When I say that abortion is the killing of another human being, I want people to believe me, to feel the weight of the issue. By my mere speech, I hope to convince. But the question is this: Am I demonstrating integrity on the issue of abortion? If I am not, I need to recognize that my words will carry little weight.

This is a tough question, and one that I might want to leave unasked. Acting with integrity on the issue of abortion may bring demands upon me that are very great—maybe more than I feel I am able to handle. For example, I know that approximately four hundred abortions will be carried out in the St. Louis area this next week. I say that every abortion is the taking of a human life. That means that I know that approximately four hundred people will be killed here in St. Louis this next week. What is more, in contrast to other crimes, I have the advantage of knowing approximately when and exactly where these murders will be committed. I also have access to the names and addresses of those who will be carrying them out. The victims are local unborn children, Americans, all of whom are alive now, and—unless someone intervenes—all of whom will be dead a week from now.

The awareness of these facts is a great and discomfiting burden to the Christian's conscience. It is a knowledge of facts of immense and awful proportion. Four hundred children to be slaughtered here next week! Does not moral integrity demand, in addition to the essential works of evangelism, adoption, opening homes to unwed mothers, and so forth, that some kind of immediate protection be given those individuals, that some action be taken—something beyond words?

We must quickly note that this argument does not say that words are insignificant. Words are essential. After all, God has communicated His truth to us through words. The point is that words can be made insignificant or empty if they are not ratified by action. Nor are we saying (as we anticipate where this argument may lead) that the "something beyond words" must always be radical, illegal activity. Any words spoken or actions taken, genuinely aimed at protecting the lives that are at risk, would display integrity, so long as the words were not out of accord with the action.

But what is a "reasonable action"? If I were somehow to learn that at a certain hour of the day my next-door neighbor planned to execute his three-year-old son, what response would I have? I would certainly do everything I could to prevent the injustice to the boy! Of course, under the present law I would call the police immediately and would expect their prompt intervention. But what if the police were not available in time to help? Or what if the police refused to come when I called, because the law provided that my neighbor had the right to choose to take his child's life if he wanted to? What if I were the only one in the neighborhood who believed that something should be done to protect my neighbor's boy?

Making the decision to intervene would likely require that I go onto my neighbor's property, or perhaps that I physically wrench the rifle from my neighbor's grasp. It probably would involve shouting and a scuffle with the would-be killer. In any case, it would involve extraordinary measures, perhaps even at substantial risk to my own safety. I might have to make quite a scene, but who could argue that this would not be totally appropriate, reasonable, and expected behavior on my part? (I need to ask myself: Would a lesser response demonstrate integrity?)

No one would need a carefully reasoned rationale for taking such extreme measures. No one needs a college course in ethics to make what is a natural, human response. Seeing a child in danger causes a visceral reaction. Anything else would be an affront to human dignity, because it is part of being human, of being made in the image of God, to have such an instinctive reaction when a human life is threatened.

But, sadly, that instinctive reaction can be suppressed. It can even be destroyed for all practical purposes, as it has been in the not-so-distant past. I recently watched on public television a lengthy documentary on the death camps in Eastern Europe, operated by Germany during World War II. The nine-hour film titled *Shoah* was composed entirely of interviews with witnesses who lived through the Holocaust, giving their recollections of what they had seen and heard. A farmer whose land was adjacent to the gas chambers and ovens at Treblinka was interviewed. He had farmed land on both sides of the railroad tracks that led to the death camp. Often, in his efforts to move farm machinery from one field to another across the tracks, he would be delayed by trains of boxcars filled with screaming Jewish men, women, and children headed for the gas chambers and ovens. He would watch—and wait for the train to pass. When the train had cleared the crossing, transporting its human cargo to the point of final destination, when the screams became more distant, this farmer would drive his tractor across the tracks and go on with his daily routine.

The film's narrator asked the farmer how it had been possible for him to continue in his daily routine when he knew that people were being tortured and slaughtered by the thousands every day right next door. If you saw the film, you know what his answer was: "If I cut my finger, it doesn't hurt him." And later in the film another witness to the slaughter responded in this way:

Q. It didn't bother him to work so near those screams?
A. At first it was unbearable; then you get used to it.
Q. You get used to anything?
A. Yes.

The "instinctive" human response to help another, even in life-and-death situations, is far from reliable. It can be suppressed; it can even be destroyed. When it is suppressed or destroyed, it is then that courses in ethics (for the Christian: objective Biblical commands and principles) become particularly crucial. Instincts, feelings, or natural responses—not just for the Polish farmer in *Shoah*, but for each of us—are very untrustworthy guides to moral integrity. Human beings have the capacity to adjust to almost any situation.

The Polish farmer's options were probably extremely limited. Was there anything he could really do to stop the horror he witnessed every day? Unarmed, against the well-guarded trains and fortress-like death camp, he was essentially helpless. Yet, even in the darkest days of the Nazi Holocaust there were some rare examples of successful intervention against impossible odds.

One of these is related by Heinz Ullstein, a Berlin Jew who had married a non-Jew. He, together with thousands of other Jewish men who had married non-Jewish wives, was arrested by the Nazis in 1943. His wife and the wives of the other prisoners stood firm in seeking their husbands' release:

> The Gestapo were preparing for large-scale action. Columns of covered trucks were drawn up at the gates of factories and stood in front of private houses. All day long they rolled through the streets, escorted by armed SS men . . . heavy vehicles under whose covers could be discerned the outlines of closely packed humanity. . . . On this day, every Jew living in Germany was arrested and for the time being lodged in mass camps. It was the beginning of the end.
>
> People lowered their eyes, some with indifference, others perhaps with a fleeting sense of horror and shame. The day wore on, there was a war to be won, provinces were conquered, "History was made," we were on intimate terms with the millennium. And the public eye missed the flickering of a tiny torch which might have kindled the fire of general resistance to despotism. From the vast collecting centers to which the Jews of Berlin had been taken, the Gestapo sorted out those with "Aryan kin" and concentrated them in a separate prison in the Rosenstrasse. No one knew what was to happen to them.
>
> At this point the wives stepped in. Already by the early hours of the next day they had discovered the whereabouts of their husbands and as by common consent, as if they had been summoned, a crowd of them appeared at the gate of the improvised detention center. In vain the security police tried to turn away the demonstrators, some 6,000 of them, and to disperse them. Again and again they massed together, advanced, called for their husbands, who despite strict instructions to

the contrary showed themselves at the windows, and demanded their release.

For a few hours the routine of a working day interrupted the demonstration, but in the afternoon the square was again crammed with people, and the demanding, accusing cries of the women rose above the noise of the traffic like passionate avowals of a love strengthened by the bitterness of life.

Gestapo headquarters was situated in the Burgstrasse, not far from the square where the demonstration was taking place. A few salvos from a machine gun could have wiped the women off the square, but the SS did not fire, not this time. Scared by an incident which had no equal in the history of the Third Reich, headquarters consented to negotiate. They spoke soothingly, gave assurances, and finally released the prisoners.[1]

Such reports of acts of nonviolent intervention during Hitler's reign are rare indeed. The Polish farmer may not have had the same opportunity. Our purpose here is not to evaluate the farmer's morals, but to recognize the amazing elasticity of the human psyche. I see myself in the Polish farmer more than in the wives of the Jewish prisoners. It is very easy to adjust. I fear that most of us, like the farmer, have adjusted to the atrocities in our neighborhoods. We go about our work pretty much as usual. Our priorities seem to be to promote peace, comfort, and security in our careers, our estates, our education, and even in our cozy churches. Perhaps because of the real cost of "calling a spade a spade," we have retreated into the shadows on the subject of abortion. But we need to remember the words of Scripture: "You are the light of the world. A city on a hill cannot be hidden. Neither do people light a lamp and put it under a bowl. Instead they put it on its stand, and it gives light to everyone in the house."[2] This Scripture is most popularly applied to, but should not be limited to, evangelism. It has particular application to ethics. In the next verse Jesus says, "In the same way, let your light shine before men, that they may see your good deeds. . . ."[3] When a Christian becomes aware of intolerable evil in his community, he is to be a lamp. He is not to retreat into a corner, nor is he to put his lamp "under a bowl." It is his job to let the light of truth shine clearly in order to expose the evil so that it will be obvious. Again, this duty can be fulfilled in the abortion controversy in hundreds of ways. Christians are men and women of individual vocation; God calls us to divergent tasks. But whatever the tasks, the salt must be salty, and the lamp must be placed on the lampstand.

Lighting the world is not a natural inclination. As fallen men, we naturally love the darkness.[4] When natural man becomes aware of an awful evil in his midst, he has an uncanny inclination to turn off the lights. Christians often follow this inclination as well. With regard to abortion, we Christians may not have turned the lights off altogether, but we have dimmed them to the point where we are having a difficult time making out some of the objects in the room.

Henry David Thoreau, though he did not claim to be a Christian, recognized the importance of acting with integrity. He wrote during the upheaval over slavery and the Mexican War, and accurately observed:

> There are thousands who are in opinion opposed to slavery and to the war, who yet in effect do nothing to put an end to them; who, esteeming themselves children of Washington and Franklin, sit down with their hands in their pockets, and say that they know not what to do, and do nothing; who even postpone the question of freedom to the question of free-trade, and quietly read the prices-current along with the latest advices from Mexico, after dinner, and, it may be, fall asleep over them both. What is the price-current of an honest man and patriot today? They hesitate, and they regret, and sometimes they petition; but they do nothing in earnest and with effect. They will wait, well disposed, for others to remedy the evil, that they may no longer have it to regret. At most, they give only a cheap vote, and a feeble countenance and Godspeed, to the right, as it goes by them.[5]

How many of us, with respect to the outrage of abortion, are waiting and hoping for others to remedy the evil, that we may no longer have it to regret? How many are frustrated, feeling the demands of conscience, and wanting to stand in the way of the evil, but not knowing what to do?

Some have successfully resisted abortion in various ways, without violating the law. But to "stand in the way" effectively, in resisting abortion law, may also mean to violate the law. *Roe v. Wade* is the law of the land. It guarantees the right to abortion. To "stand in the way" on the abortion issue means to intervene on behalf of the unborn child, first by persuasion, but if that fails, to forbid the right to abortion. Since the Supreme Court of the United States ruled in 1973 that it is illegal to forbid the right to abortion, it is not realistic to imagine that we will be able to avoid a head-to-head conflict at some level.

In recent years some have stood in the way. Some have done this at the abortion clinic, by pressing the issue with individual women about to abort their children. Through literature, placards, and sidewalk counseling, many children have been protected without a violation of the law. But others have gone further, interposing themselves between the abortionist and his victim. They have blocked doors of abortion clinics, attempting to forbid entrance to the mother and her unborn child, to prevent the murder of the child. They have blocked doors in attempting to keep the doctor from entering, to keep him from his grim plans for the day. Some have gone even further; they have entered the abortionist's clinic and attempted to dismantle the machinery designed to destroy the children.

Of course, when people have done these things, they have broken laws. As a result, they have been arrested, prosecuted, and often fined or jailed for their offense. Almost universally, and expectedly, they have been publicly condemned by the abortion clinic personnel themselves and by the unbelieving world. Evangelical Christians have, as a rule, also roundly criticized these "radicals." A few may give them a tip of the hat for their intentions, for their commitment. But few will publicly agree that what they are doing is right. Big mainstream "right-to-life" groups keep themselves as far from such people as possible, fearing legal entanglements and not wanting the stigma of being connected with these wild-eyed folks. The activists are advised by those in the mainstream to spend their time and money in "more productive" ways— attempting to get the laws changed, attempting to sway public opinion, writing letters to the editor, getting out the right vote on election day. But they are chastised for breaking the law.

Are these people who break the law in this way right, or are they wrong? By definition, they are apparently wrong in the eyes of the civil and criminal law. But are they ultimately right or wrong?

Before we go further in finding answers to that question, meet four of these "radicals": ChristyAnne Collins, Ann O'Brien, Joan Andrews, and Joe Wall.

THREE

STANDING IN THE WAY

ChristyAnne Collins lives right near the nation's capital. She is a member of a large evangelical Episcopalian church and heads the Sanctity of Life Ministries in Annandale, Virginia. This ministry attempts to bring Bible-based values to all aspects of the abortion issue by providing services to women in crisis pregnancies and by mobilizing the Church to action.

Sanctity of Life Ministries, in an effort to provide real help to women considering or having already undergone abortions, provides counseling, medical care, pregnancy testing, post-abortion counseling, housing, financial assistance, and clothing for mother and baby.

In its effort to involve the community and Church in active opposition to abortion, Sanctity of Life Ministries helps to organize sidewalk counseling, picketing, legislative action, prayer and intercession, rescue missions, operation of a "life van" mobile counseling unit, and special events such as Mother's Day marches, prayer vigils, hospital boycotts, marches for life, and high school oratorical competitions.

It is the rescue missions that have gotten ChristyAnne Collins into some trouble. By Spring 1988, when her story was publicized as the cover story in the *Washington Post* magazine,[1] she had been arrested twenty-eight times for her efforts to intervene directly on behalf of the unborn at abortion clinics, located mostly in the Washington, D.C. and adjacent Virginia areas. Since then, she has been arrested several more times and has spent many months in jail.

On one occasion, ChristyAnne Collins stood in a hallway

outside the offices of an abortion clinic within the District of Columbia in order to give women considering abortion information about positive alternatives. She was arrested, charged with "unlawful entry," found guilty, and convicted on that charge by Judge Richard Salzman of the District of Columbia Superior Court. When she appeared for sentencing on May 16, 1988, Judge Salzman asked her if there was anything she wished to say before he pronounced sentence. The transcript records ChristyAnne's response:

Your Honor, there are several comments I would like to make. The first is that you cannot rehabilitate people from doing something good, you cannot rehabilitate people from resisting evil.

My second comment regards the presentence report issued by my probation officer (particularly her recommendation for psychiatric evaluation and ongoing psychological counseling).

I can't help but marvel. Most of the people sitting in the front row of this courtroom earn their living from the abortion industry. If I did to an animal what this Court sanctions their doing to children, you would call me mentally deranged. Yet, because I know and act as if these aborted children are not merely globs of tissue, but children made in the image of God, and because I resent seeing them reduced to arms and legs, smashed skulls, eyeballs and broken rib cages, I am the one you seek to punish and deter and subject to psychiatric evaluation.

I know abortion is the brutal murder of a baby, and have made the decision I would rather face any sanction this Court could impose upon me for resisting that evil rather than have to live with my heart, mind and soul if I were to comply with what this Court expects me to do . . . become a silent, accepting observer of the murder.

When I realize my failure to comply puts me and not them at the point of psychiatric evaluation, I know there is something terribly, terribly wrong. May God forgive.

Your Honor, you have, throughout our trial, talked about the laws of this land. The fundamental right of every American citizen is the right to life; a right our Constitution[2] declares an unalienable right endowed by our Creator. It is not something you or I or the State can choose to give or take away.

Whether a person is preborn, dying of AIDS, mentally incompe-

tent, retarded, physically handicapped or otherwise not perfect, or unwanted by some, life is not something we can choose to throw away
or minimize.

We have seen the time when, in our society, blacks, by the mere
color of their skin, were told they were not human beings. They could
be separated from their families, beaten, sold or killed. These actions
were entirely sanctioned by the courts, who denied their personhood
and were resisted by men and women who knew the law was evil.

We have seen times in our history when people, because of their
nationality [Jewish] were brutalized in concentration camps and condemned to die in gas ovens. And even today—40 years after the holocaust events, we have a world of people still seeking to punish those
responsible.

Today, throughout the world, people are looking at Kurt Waldheim
of Austria. We say, "That man should have done something." We say
he shouldn't have simply followed orders simply because the law
allowed brutality; we say he should have resisted because he knew the
acts were evil.

In the 40 years since the events of the Nazi holocaust, there are
many who believe [Waldheim] should still be held accountable for his
failure to do right and for his participation in the state-sanctioned evil.
Will the same be said of us who have for so long accepted the murder
of our children?

Your Honor, I want you to know I respect the law greatly. I respect
the law that says every human being, every American citizen, has the
unalienable right to life. I am not called to yield my conscience to the
legislature and I am not called to elevate the state to the place of God
in my life.

If the laws of this courtroom and the laws of the land that sanction
the brutal murder of an unborn child become more important than the
fact that these children are made in the image of God, and are children
He would protect, then I will have failed at what is most important in
my life: obedience to God.

I am terrified to walk through those doors into your jail, Your
Honor, and I don't mind telling you that. I am not an evil person. I
am not a criminal. And I do not belong in your jail, except under your
standard of justice which protects murder and convicts those who act
in defense of life.

I am a person who cares a whole lot for other people. I know when I walk through that door into your jail, life is going to be painful for me.

Yet it will not be nearly as painful as if I had freedom on the outside because of refusing to live by my conscience. To have the freedom to go about my daily business because I am afraid of the consequences the law might impose for resisting, would leave me a pretty empty human being.

Finally, Your Honor, I want to say the day is going to come when you and I and the abortionists sitting on the front row of this courtroom are going to stand before a different Judge. Today I face temporal consequences for my action to love and protect preborn children. I am willing to do that.

I would far rather pay any consequence you can impose upon me for my commitment to loving these children and their mothers, than to one day face the Righteous Judge and have to say I was not faithful to the call of Christ.

I cannot change who I am, Your Honor. Indeed, I would not want to be any different than I am in regard to this issue. As I said, you cannot rehabilitate me from loving women who are devastated by their abortion decisions and trying to prevent other women from making the same destructive decisions.

If refusal to act on their behalf is rehabilitation, I don't want it. I can only say to you and the other people you represent—your colleagues; officers of the court; Ms. McHenry, my prosecutor; and those sitting in the front row representing the abortion industry—the day is going to come when you will all face that different Judge.

When that day comes, I want you to know I and most of the people in this courtroom will be praying for each of you that you will come to a reconciliation between right and wrong and have given your allegiance to God's justice.

That is all I have to say, Your Honor.

Whereupon, Judge Salzman fined ChristyAnne Collins $150 and sentenced her to nine months in jail. But the judge did attempt to "soften" the sentence somewhat—he suspended five of those nine months of imprisonment on just one condition: that ChristyAnne Collins would agree to cease her activities in the halls and doorways of abortion clinics for a period of two years, under supervised probation.

ChristyAnne politely declined the offer.

Ann O'Brien is a young grandmother from St. Louis who has been involved in the pro-life effort since the 1973 *Roe v. Wade* decision. She has committed her life to anti-abortion activities. She has spoken publicly on the subject, distributed pro-life literature, supported pro-life candidates for political office, gone to the nation's capital each January for many years to join in the pro-life march, and much, much more.

But Ann has also spent a significant amount of her time, during the last ten years, in jail. She has made the decision that the unborn child is in need of "direct intervention"; that is, that she must do what she can to prevent the actual killing of the child at the point in time when the child's life is about to be taken. Ann "stands in the way" at the abortion clinics, and she has gotten into a great deal of trouble. She has been arrested for trespass, violation of court injunctions, and similar offenses hundreds of times. She is usually tried and convicted, and often jailed.

One such trial was on November 26, 1984, in St. Louis County Circuit Court. Here is the transcript of the testimony and evidence that sent her to jail on that occasion:[3]

[Direct examination by Mr. Richard Bender, attorney for the abortion clinic, specially appointed to prosecute Ann O'Brien for contempt of court for violation of a court injunction ordering her to stay off the abortion clinic property.]

Q. Please state your name.

A. Sandra Smythe.

The Court: Keep your voice up, please.

Q. (By Mr. Bender): Mrs. Smythe, please talk up as if I was in the back of the courtroom. Okay?

A. Okay.

Q. Are you currently employed?

A. Yes. Women's Clinical Group.

Q. Roitman Palmer's Women's Clinical Group?

A. Yes.

Q. How long have you been with them?

A. Seven years.

Q. Can you tell us basically what your job title and function is?

A. I am office manager.

Q. Have you been office manager for the past three or four months at least?

A. Yes, sir.

Q. Now, in connection with the office, can you tell us where it is located?

A. It is at 3394 McKelvey, and we are in Suite 111.

Q. And as far as the building itself, can you describe the building, please?

A. It has offices around an atrium, and we are on the east side.

Q. How many offices are there inside the building itself?

A. I think around thirteen; twelve or thirteen.

Q. And they're all individual suites?

A. Yes, sir.

Q. And you are in Suite 111?

A. Yes, sir.

Q. Does anybody else occupy the suite besides the Roitman Palmer Women's Clinical Group, Incorporated?

A. No, sir.

Q. And it is a corporation; correct?

A. Yes, sir.

Q. Now as far as the entrance to the clinical group, is there a door that you enter to get into the clinical group itself?

A. Yes, sir.

Q. And does that door open up from the atrium?

A. Yes, sir.

Q. Is there another door to the main entrance to the building?

A. Yes, sir.

Q. All right. And is it—can you describe—you enter the main entrance; and then is there a walkway to yours?

A. Yes, sir. There is an entrance on both sides. And then you walk through the atrium to get to our condominium.

Q. Is there a sidewalk that leads from the main walkway to your individual suite?

A. Yes, sir.

Q. And how long is the walkway, from the sidewalk to the individual suite?

A. I'd say maybe three feet.

Q. And then as far as the office itself; once you walk inside the door, are you inside the office?

A. No.

Q. What is there?

A. The waiting room is first; and then you walk through another door, and you're into the office area, into the examining rooms and everything.

Q. So there is one door that takes you into the waiting room?

A. Yes, sir.

Q. And a second door from the waiting room into the offices themselves?

A. Yes, sir.

Q. And once you get inside the offices themselves, are there individual offices, examining rooms or such?

A. Yes, sir.

Q. Okay. Now were you present in court back on October 1st when this Court had a hearing concerning a preliminary or temporary injunction?

A. Yes, sir.

Q. Were you present in court that entire time?

A. Yes, sir.

Q. Were you also in court on October 3rd when there were criminal contempt hearings?

A. Yes, sir.

Q. Were you present in court that entire day also?

A. Yes, sir.

Q. And were you in court on October 1st when the Honorable Judge Campbell entered an order concerning the restraining and enjoining of certain defendants from certain activities?

[OBJECTIONS; OVERRULED]

A. Yes, sir.

Q. And did you have an opportunity at that time to know any of the individuals on that day that were seated in the jury box [as defendants]?

A. Yes, sir, I did.

Q. And are you familiar with Ann O'Brien?

A. Yes, sir.

Q. And did you observe her in the jury box on October 1st and October 3rd?

[OBJECTIONS; OVERRULED]

A. Yes, sir; I did see her. . . .

Q. Do you observe her in the courtroom today?

A. Yes, sir.

Q. And can you point her out for the Court, please?

A. The gray headed lady sitting behind the lawyer.

Q. The gray haired individual sitting at the counsel table?

A. Yes, sir.

* * * *

Q. Now as far as the office at McKelvey Avenue; did you have any orders attached to the door, or the window next to the door?

A. Yes, sir; and also had one at the entrance doors, too.

Q. All right. And as far as the orders that have been attached to the doors, have you read those orders?

A. Yes, sir.

Q. And are you familiar with the signature that purports to be on the bottom of those orders?

A. Yes, sir.

Q. And whose signature does that purport to be?

A. Judge Campbell's.

Q. And when you say you have those on the doors to the building, can you tell us where they're located?

A. Right. When you come in the double glass doors, it is right on the door itself.

Q. And as far as the office door that leads into your individual suite, Suite 111, can you tell us where the order is posted?

A. Right beside the door on the glass.

Q. And was the order affixed to the door on November 8th?

A. Yes, sir.

Q. Now on November 8th can you tell us when you first observed Mrs. O'Brien?

A. It was about 12:15 when one of our patients came in. And she kept saying, "Get this woman away from me. Get her away."

Q. All right. And as far as Mrs. O'Brien, did she come through the door that leads to the office suite?

A. She came into the one through the waiting room, and also through the office one.

Q. And so she came through the second door into the offices next?

A. Yes, sir.

Q. And did you observe her saying anything to anyone?

A. Yes, sir.

Q. And was there a patient that she was with?

A. She was—

Q. Next to?

A. Yes.

Q. Without telling me anything about the patient, could you recall anything that Mrs. O'Brien was doing or saying? Could you describe what you observed?

A. She was yelling and screaming at her.

Q. And do you recall what she was saying?

A. Yes, sir.

Q. And what did she say?

A. "Please don't murder your baby."

Q. Anything else?

A. No. Just kept saying we were murderers, and to please not go in there.

Q. And did you ask Mrs. O'Brien to leave?

A. Yes, sir.

Q. And upon your request did she leave immediately?

A. No, sir. She just kept yelling.

Q. And did you advise her she was violating a Court order?

A. Yes, sir. I told her she wasn't supposed to be in there.

Q. Was anybody else present at the office?

A. The other office employees.

Q. All right. Did anyone assist the patient in any way?

A. Yes, sir. One of the girls did.

Q. All right. What did they do?

A. They had to take her in the back and get her calmed down. She was crying and upset.

Q. Can you tell us the condition that you observed the patient in? What was she doing during this period?

A. She was hysterical.

Q. When you say hysterical, crying?

A. Yes, sir.

Q. And Mrs. O'Brien, during this period of time, was continuing to, you say, yell and scream?

Mr. Finnegan: Objection, Your Honor; the question is leading.

The Court: Objection sustained.

A. She was still yelling and screaming. . . .

Mr. Finnegan: Objection, Your Honor; the question is leading.

The Court: Objection sustained.

Mr. Bender: I will rephrase it.

Q. (By Mr. Bender) And what was Mrs. O'Brien doing during this period of time?

A. She was still standing there yelling and screaming at the patient.

Q. And did you ever advise her that you were going to call the police?

A. Yes, sir.

Q. And did you in fact call the Bridgeton Police?

A. Yes, sir, we did.

Q. And where was Mrs. O'Brien when you called the Bridgeton Police?

A. Standing right there.

Q. Still inside the offices?

A. Yes, sir.

Q. All right. And did she subsequently leave the office?

A. Finally, she did.

Q. Approximately how long was she inside the office that all this occurred?

A. I'd say around five minutes.

Q. And did the Bridgeton Police subsequently come and arrest her?

A. Yes, sir.

Q. Did you observe the Bridgeton Police arrive shortly thereafter?

A. Yes, sir.

Q. About how long thereafter was it?

A. Just a couple of minutes.

Q. And did they take her away?

A. Yes, sir.

Mr. Bender: That is all I have of this witness, Your Honor.

[After the attorneys conferred in chambers with the Court, when defense motions were argued to the Court and overruled, and when the defense informed the Court that the defendant would not put on any evidence in her own behalf, the proceedings were concluded]:

The Court: Let the record show that I find that Ann O'Brien is guilty of indirect criminal contempt of court.

I find the defendant had actual knowledge of the terms and conditions of the temporary injunction by being present in court when same was read to defendants.

In addition, the temporary injunction was posted prominently in two places. It is not part of my judgment, but she was also represented by counsel here at the hearing at the time of the conditions of the temporary injunction.

I find that on November 8, 1984, between the hours of 12:00 noon and 2:00 p.m. she willfully violated the temporary injunction by entering the premises known as and numbered 3394 McKelvey Avenue, and even entering Suite 111 thereof; and by interfering with a patient's ingress to the premises; and did then and there refuse to leave after being so requested by plaintiff's office manager.

I find all of this beyond a reasonable doubt. I find that her actions were willful and deliberate violations of the temporary injunction issued by this Court after due notice of all contents.

And I find that she has committed indirect criminal contempt of court.

Accordingly, it is ordered, adjudged and decreed that defendant Ann O'Brien is guilty of indirect criminal contempt of this Court by willfully, deliberately and knowingly violating the temporary injunction of this Court after notice thereof.

Defendant Ann O'Brien is hereby sentenced to serve a term of three months in custody of the St. Louis County Department of Justice Services.

In addition, Defendant Ann O'Brien is sentenced to pay a fine of $500.00. And defendant's cash bond in said amount is applied to said fine.

Defendant Ann O'Brien is committed and remanded immediately to the St. Louis County Department of Justice Services without bond. And, on the record, I will give a copy of the Warrant and Order of Commitment to the Department of Justice Services at this time. . . .

That concludes the record.

Ann O'Brien does not believe that she was wrong in entering the abortion clinic, even though she knew that the judge had ordered her not to. Although she denies privately that she was "screaming and yelling," she does agree that she did everything she could to convince the female patient, who was seeking an abortion, to change her mind, and that her talking visibly upset the patient. Ann believed then—and she believes now—that her actions were right, and that they were appropriate to the matter at hand: a baby's life was about to be taken. Ann believes it is appropriate that a mother, about to kill her child, should be confronted and, if necessary, upset. Ann believes that it is wholly inappropriate to stand aside and pretend that anything short of a murder is going on inside the abortion clinic.

Joan Andrews has spent much of her recent life in jail. To date, her longest single period of imprisonment was about two-and-one-half years, most of which was in solitary confinement. This incarceration was a result of her July 1986 trial and conviction on a charge of attempted burglary in the Escambia County, Florida Circuit Court. She had entered The Ladies' Center, a Pensacola abortion clinic, in March of that year. Once inside the clinic, she had attempted to disable the clinic's suction machine, an instrument used by the abortionist to force the baby out of the uterus, ripping the baby's body apart and taking its life.

After her conviction in July, and after a presentence investigation had been compiled and presented, Judge William Anderson sentenced her to five years, the maximum allowed by law for the offense and double the thirty month maximum set out in Florida's sentencing guidelines.[4] (Joan was released from confinement on October 19, 1988, after her supporters had flooded the Florida governor's office with requests for her release. The governor finally yielded to the pressure and signed an order commuting her sentence.)

Her presentence report recounted the act that resulted in the court's decision to order the five years of imprisonment:

Information received from the Pensacola Police Department arrest report indicates that on 3/26/86, at approximately 10:14 a.m., Officer William L. Horn, #223, of the Pensacola Police Department, responded to a Disturbance Call at 6770 N. 9th Avenue, Pensacola, Florida (Ladies Center). Officer Horn observed the subject (Joan Elizabeth Andrews) enter the Ladies Center by running up the stairs and through the door on the south side of the occupied dwelling. The subject failed to stop when Officer Horn commanded her and the other subjects to stop. Ms. Andrews ran up the stairs and into the room on the southeast corner. Ms. Andrews was grabbing and pulling on equipment when she was placed under arrest. Ms. Andrews was pulling on an electrical cord and one piece of equipment when she was placed under arrest. Ms. Andrews refused to let go of the cord when requested by Officer Horn. Ms. Andrews had to be pried loose from the equipment and had to be physically subdued and carried to the police vehicle.[5]

March 26, 1986, was not the first time Joan Andrews had been arrested. Since 1973, she had dedicated her entire career to pro-life activities and had been arrested hundreds of times. She had received many convictions for trespassing, "loitering," violating court injunctions to remain off abortion clinic properties, and similar misdemeanors and petty offenses. She had been arrested in Missouri, Delaware, Pennsylvania, Maryland, and other states. It was because of this kind of record, of which Judge Anderson was advised, that his sentence was stiff. The judge entered an order in her case explaining his reasons:

ORDER SETTING FORTH REASONS FOR
DEPARTURE FROM SENTENCING GUIDELINES

This defendant has a long record of trespasses and invasions of the property of others, which is of escalating seriousness. The record and the defendant's own statements disclose that for several years her only business has been the going from state to state for the purpose of committing such criminal acts. The defendant has consistently advised the Court that she would not obey the conditions of any probation, but unless confined she will continue to commit further criminal acts, as she is not bound by the laws that bind others. For these reasons, no probation, community control, or lenient sentence will serve to end her criminal conduct, and a lengthy period of incarceration is necessary.[6]

Joan firmly believes that the sentence was immoral; she believes that any sentence would have been immoral. She firmly believes that her actions were right, and that Judge Anderson, as well as the 1973 Supreme Court, was wrong. But she would not argue with much of the substance of what the judge said in his explanation. She does have a long history of trespass convictions. She would admit that she had gone from state to state for several years to attempt to stop abortions in ways that were contrary to the civil law, many times intentionally violating orders of the court in that locality. She told Judge Anderson that if she were given probation she could not abide by its terms, which would be in part that she stay away from abortion clinics and cease her illegal activities. Joan would agree, not generally that "she is not bound by the laws that bind others," but particularly that neither her conscience nor moral Law (which God has proclaimed) would permit her to be bound by a law that required her to abstain from attempting to restrain a doctor from performing an abortion. Joan believes that she has a duty to intervene for the unborn child on the day of his appointment for death, and sees that particular duty as superior to any duty she has to obey the civil law which forbids trespass. Whenever the civil law stands in the way of obedience to her moral duty, she can take no other action.

Joe Wall turned sixty not long ago. Until September 1986 he was employed as a senior auditor in the Philadelphia City Controller's office. Joe was a career man. He had worked in that office for twenty years. But in September 1986 he lost his job. His supervisor would not approve his request for "vacation time" when Joe was jailed because a court found that he had violated the terms of his probation arising out of a conviction of trespassing on the property of an abortion clinic. Although he had forty-eight vacation days available, his supervisor chose to exercise his discretion in the matter, denying Joe's application and releasing him as "AWOL" after five days in jail.

Joe Wall had joined fourteen other pro-lifers on May 10, 1985, when they entered an abortion clinic in Pittsburgh. The facility, the Women's Health Services Abortion Clinic, is reputed to be the third-largest abortion clinic in the United States, with an average of about fifty killings per day. All fifteen of the protesters were arrested. Joe was charged with defiant trespass, criminal mischief, resisting arrest (all misdemeanors), and criminal trespass (a felony). The Allegheny County District Attorney's office prosecuted his case. The case was tried by a jury in November 1985. He was found guilty of defiant trespass and criminal trespass, and although he spent more than two months in jail immediately following his conviction, Judge Novak, the presiding judge at the trial, then put him on probation. One of the terms of his probation was that he not trespass at abortion clinics.

In 1986, the prosecution asked Judge Novak to revoke Joe Wall's probation and to put him in jail, claiming that he had violated the terms of his probation by trespassing at abortion clinics once again. Joe was commanded to appear before Judge Novak for a hearing on the matter. He appeared, and the following is a partial transcript of those proceedings:

The Court: Mr. Wall, would you come forward with counsel, please. Mr. Wall, the law requires that I give you an opportunity to address the Court prior to sentencing. Is there anything you would like to say?

The Defendant: Yes. I thank you. Good morning, Your Honor. When my attorney told me I had a right to a presentencing allocution, I prepared a long and, frankly, rather verbose analysis of the prosecution and the trial. However, thinking it over I decided to chuck it. The hour is late, metaphorically speaking, and the time for that is past. There are more important things than raking over old coals. Those who have followed this trial understand what went on, I feel certain. Those who have eyes to see, have seen. Enough said on that.

Now that the legal process has ended, we can dispense with the pretense, with the sham that this prosecution had nothing to do with the subject of abortion. This was the substantive issue; everyone in this courtroom knows it. It is time we addressed it. The only reason we went into that clinic that day was to attempt to stop the killing, the murder, of innocent unborn children. It beggars common sense to say that fifteen people would walk into a clinic and stay there for no reason at all. If they did so, they should have had a sanity hearing, not a trial. I know I would not have been there, nor would I be here today, for any other reason, given my age, fifty-nine, my bad heart, my professional background.

I, and the other fourteen of us went into that abortion clinic to take one small step to help fight an evil so immense that it is hard to grasp, difficult to comprehend. And that is a large part of the problem. Most people can't comprehend it; they don't even want to think about it.

Just for a moment, think about it. Twenty million or more human beings killed since 1973. Torn to pieces, shredded into garbage, burned to death. That's the reality we have to live with, to try to face. We are constantly reminded of the terrible Nazi Holocaust, it's engraved on our collective memory. "Never again," we say. I remember the Nazi Holocaust; I was a young soldier during World War Two. It was a horrible thing. But what about the American Holocaust? We are in the middle of it right now. The Nazis killed eleven million in their holocaust; we Americans have slaughtered over twenty million, with no end in sight. Twice as many; thrice as many.

In the face of an incredible tragedy like this, any charges of trespass shrink into insignificance. To say that, in attempting to halt this blood bath, we must blindly and mindlessly follow the letter of the law, without regard to whether it is just or not, among other things makes a mockery of our whole American history, our struggle for freedom. Our founding fathers—Washington, Jefferson, Franklin—broke the civil law of a legitimate government of the day. Can we castigate them, to regard them as common criminals? Later, in the days of the underground railway, the Quakers and others who operated it broke the law—they stole another man's property—for which they were detested by the southern slaveholders. In passing, I might add that the Federal Fugitive Slave Act, a perfectly legal act of Congress, was largely ignored by northern officials, including governors, judges, and sheriffs. It's an unjust and immoral law, they said, and we refuse to enforce it. Later, in our own day, we have the example of Doctor Martin Luther King. Dr. King broke the law to bring attention to the unjust and immoral legal structure which degraded and offended the human dignity of our Black fellow citizens. If we followed the logic given in this trial, he was no better than a common trespasser. Well, today, we find this "common trespasser," if you will—actually a very brave and humane man— being honored with a national holiday. Doesn't that tell something about the nature of his deeds?

The point of this is that the idea that you can separate a particular action in technical violation of the law from the reason for it makes no sense whatever. For one who thinks that way, a major portion of American history is no more than a criminal conspiracy.

Now, as to why we did what we did—I can only speak for myself. I am a Catholic, I believe in the truth of the Catholic faith, I have an obligation to follow that faith, regardless of where it leads. It's not something that's optional; if I believe in it, I must follow it to the end. As an illustration of what I mean, let me quote from Thomas More, at his trial, when he told the judges: ". . . ye must understand that, in things touching conscience, every true and good subject is more bound to have respect to his said conscience and to his soul than to any other thing in all the world beside . . ." (*Trial of St. Thomas More*, E. Reynolds). Our Catholic faith teaches us that we have a real, basic obligation to help the weak; to, as the Scriptures say, ". . . rescue those being dragged to the slaughter." We simply can't ignore this, pretend it isn't there. To do so is a sin of omission. The parable of the Good Samaritan is not a pious fable; it is an order, a binding directive as to how we should act when we find one of our fellow human beings in danger of injury or death. That day at the abortion clinic, fifty human beings were about to be murdered. Every Catholic, every Christian in the City of Pittsburgh, from Bishop Bevillaqua on down, including you, Judge Novak, should have been there to help us stop these murders. I can't answer for their consciences, but I have to answer for mine. And mine told me I had to be there to stop these killings. I don't apologize for this. I was there, I am glad I was there.

We may or may not have stopped any killing, but we tried. As Mother Teresa of Calcutta has said, "We are not called upon to be successful, but we are called upon to be faithful." Those fifteen of us who went to the Women's Health Services Abortion Clinic that day tried—in our own fumbling, inept way—to be faithful.

That's all we could do. And I'm glad we did it.

The Court: Mr. Wall, at the time of your bond hearing, consideration of bond, I explained to you as carefully as I could my responsibilities under the criminal law which I am sworn to uphold.

I indicated to you at that time that under our system of government you have a right to protest against any law with which you disagree. I explained to you that there was a difference between your right to protest and your right to speak out and your right to just move beyond that border line of protest, and infraction of criminal law, namely, to trespass.

It is obvious that you know where that line is because your protest would have no symbolism if you did not move over that line and cause the situation where the police were forced to react to your presence in that facility.

My question of you is simply this: You have been arrested many times. Presentence report indicates, correct me if it is incorrect—

The Defendant: Fifteen times, Your Honor.

The Court: —that you have been arrested in St. Louis, Wilmington, Philadelphia, Cherry Hill, New Jersey; is that correct?

The Defendant: That's correct.

The Court: Now, all of these arrests took place prior to your trial in this court.

The Defendant: That's right.

The Court: At the time that I spoke to you after the trial, I placed upon you a condition that you not trespass upon facilities which perform abortions.

The Defendant: That's right.

The Court: You indicated to me that you could not in good conscience comply with that condition of bond which simply applied to criminal law. Is that correct?

The Defendant: That's right.

The Court: Subsequent to that time, I was petitioned to reconsider for bond and I did, indicating that you could be released if you would promise not to trespass upon facilities which perform abortions and you signed a certification that you would in fact not do so between your conviction and today's hearing.

The Defendant: That's right.

The Court: Now, have you, as the District Attorney alleges you have, trespassed?

The Defendant: I have not been convicted of any trespass of any abortion facilities, Your Honor.

The Court: That's obvious. It would be impossible for you to be convicted because justice doesn't move that quickly. My question is: Have you been arrested for the same behavior which brought you before this Court, whether or not you believe they are lawful?

The Defendant: I was arrested. Some of the cases were thrown out. I have every confidence that the others will be for trespassing on grounds, not on abortion facilities. I do this continually.

The Court: Well, so that we don't mince words, Mr. Wall, did you enter upon a facility that performs abortions and lock yourself in one of the procedure rooms?

The Defendant: No, I did not.

The Court: You did enter upon such facility?

The Defendant: I entered a building that was owned by—where an abortion clinic was situated. I never got to the actual procedure room.

The Court: Why not?

The Defendant: Because the elevators wouldn't work, and I could not get up the stairs.

The Court: Let's get to this decision. Did something happen between the date we spoke, the date of trial, and the date that you signed that condition of bond to change your mind about the form of your protest?

The Defendant: No, I felt when I thought it over what we were doing is covered legally and that is not considered to be trespass. It is covered by justification. We have a legal right to do that under justification. It is a perfectly legal thing to do. As far as I was concerned, anything we did along these lines is covered by the doctrine of justification. It is not illegal. What will happen, one of these days we come to court and allow justification, or an appeal in this particular case might very well obtain justification. Therefore, we did not do anything illegal. I don't mean that my conscience would be troubled by that. If it troubled my conscience, I wouldn't sign that.

The Court: If this Court were to place you on probation and the condition of probation would be that you not enter upon the premises of a facility which performs abortions, would you abide by that condition?

The Defendant: I could only answer, Your Honor, that I have to follow my conscience. Everybody in here has a right to follow their conscience. I don't know what the circumstances would be, but you would have to suppose a child or person was screaming, up in a burning building—I couldn't go in there because it was an abortion facility? I don't answer that. I will follow my conscience. We all have to do that.

The Court: Do you intend to engage in the same behavior after this conviction as you engaged in before?

The Defendant: I can't speak for the future, Your Honor. I can only say whatever comes, I will depend on my conscience. What happens at that time, I can't say. I have no knowledge of the future. I intend to follow my conscience, Your Honor.

The Court: Mr. Wall, the beliefs which you hold are very deep. I told you before and I will tell you again, I respect you for the power and the depth of your convictions. You believe that this was the case about abortion, the right to life. As I told you, from the point of view of the law, this case is a much lesser issue, a case of trespass.

I think that the nature of your speaking out against abortion has caused you to believe that it is necessary for you to move over that line and disobey the law which encourages the justification processes, arrest, arraignment, bail, pretrial hearings, post-trial motion hearings and now sentence.

Obviously, you make a conscious decision that this is necessary because you believe you are acting in behalf of the higher good.

The Defendant: We also believe we are acting in conjunction with the law. We believe our actions are completely legal and the courts will prove them to be legal. We are not lawbreakers. We are not violating the law.

The Court: If that's so, then those who believe otherwise would enter your home and protest in that manner.

The Defendant: If I were about to kill somebody in my home, I would hope somebody came in and stopped me.

The Court: If those who believed in the freedom of choice to have an abortion were able to carry out their convictions the same way as you, they would be free to trespass upon your property and we would have a war of rights, one trespassing against another.

The Defendant: We are in a civil war right now. Twenty million people have been killed. The war is going on right now. It is happening right now. It is before our eyes. Only the blind cannot see.

The Court: I see exactly what you are saying. I understand what you are saying, Mr. Wall. I believe, however, that your protest against performance of abortion must be conducted just as any other movement within this country and that is within the boundaries set by the law. One of those boundaries is a very simple law, the law of trespass. You were found by a jury of your peers to have violated that law or these laws.

You cannot assure this Court that you will not enter upon facilities of the abortion clinics to halt the performance of abortions?

The Defendant: I can only assure that I will follow my conscience.

The Court: You were following your conscience on the day that you were arrested on matters that brought you before this Court?

The Defendant: That's correct.

The Court: Well, Mr. Wall, God knows, you answered to higher authority than I. You are very sincere in the following of your convictions. I think you are very brave. I have taken note of your heart condition, but as you testified to the jury, you entered upon that facility within weeks of your open heart surgery, knowing that you would cause yourself to be arrested as a result of your protest.

For the offense of criminal trespass, you are sentenced to a period of incarceration for no less than six, nor more than twelve months at the Mercer facility. You are sentenced to a period of probation of three years. I find that the crime of defiant trespass merges with the crime of criminal trespass for the purposes of sentence. You are to pay the costs of prosecution.

Joe Wall appealed Judge Novak's order to the Pennsylvania Superior Court. After over eighteen months, that court affirmed Judge Novak. Now Joe has appealed the case to the Pennsylvania Supreme Court (the highest court in Pennsylvania), and if he fails there, plans to take the case to the federal courts, since he believes that substantial constitutional issues are involved.

Joe does not want to go to jail. He hates jail. He did not want to be fired from his job. He liked his job. The irony is that in all likelihood, Joe could avoid any future jail time if he would go back into Judge Novak's courtroom and tell the judge that he would agree not to trespass in the future at any abortion clinic's property. Judge Novak would be happy with him if he did so. Most would think of him as a good, law-abiding citizen if he would do that simple act. It would make it so much easier on Joe, on his family, on the courts, on the pro-life lawyers like Theresa Connolly in Philadelphia who is representing Joe on his appeal without charge. The people at the abortion clinic would appreciate Joe's good sense too. It certainly would make their work go more smoothly.

But there are fifty little people headed toward the Women's Health Services Abortion Clinic in Pittsburgh next Monday, or Tuesday, or any day next week who are very much in need of Joe's help. From their perspective, Joe's actions—though they may have been performed in his own "fumbling, inept way"—were fit and suitable to the occasion.

WHAT SCRIPTURE SAYS

W ere these four citizens right in what they did, or were they wrong? Or were they somewhere in between? Of course, they were all guilty of violating the civil law. If violation of the civil law is always wrong, then they were wrong. If there are areas in which a Christian can disobey the civil law, was this one of those areas? That is, were these four anti-abortionists right or wrong as judged by Scripture?

This is not a question that is limited to ChristyAnne Collins, Ann O'Brien, Joan Andrews, and Joe Wall. Evangelical Christians in increasing numbers have been expressing opposition to abortion through actions similar to these four. Their actions range from confronting the abortion patients on sidewalks in front of the abortion clinics, to sitting in front of the abortion clinic's doors to block entrance, to gaining access to the abortion clinic itself and "sitting in" on the floor of the waiting room to prevent the doctors at the clinic from doing any abortions for a period of time. In some cases, such as that of Joan Andrews, it even involves the attempted dismantling of equipment to force a temporary shutdown of the business. But it always involves nonviolent yet confrontational intervention at the abortion clinic itself, where the action taken violates the law.[1]

In all likelihood, the Christian reader already has put together some feelings, and probably some judgments, about the four we have discussed. Some will almost certainly judge them to be wrong (although well-motivated), because they violated the law, and because in the American Christian community it is widely assumed that the Christian has an absolute duty to obey the civil law. Some will instinctively feel repulsed by the actions of Joan, Ann,

ChristyAnne, and Joe because they appear to be attempting to impose the Christian's moral code on other people. It is judged that Christians ought not do so, but ought rather to seek accomplishment of their goals through prayer, preaching, and persuasion. They should not repeat the mistakes of the Crusades and Constantine, who tried to inflict Christianity, or the mores of the Christian faith, on others. Still others will see these four as cast in the same mold as the "radicals" who protested against the military draft, or who protested for other, less noble reasons in the sixties and seventies. And yet there are a few Christians who would agree with these four, who believe they did what was right.

But what does Scripture say?[2] It is essential that Scripture be examined carefully on the subject. Christians cannot make judgments based on feelings, nor is it safe to characterize another Christian as a "type" without examining his motivations, his rationale, and his concerns. A Christian's only rule of faith and practice is the Word of God. What should the Christian do when the world confronts him with a moral or ethical quandary, forcing a decision, perhaps in uncharted water? He should go to Scripture. When his conscience frustrates him, compelling a decision, he examines God's Word. His conscience is not isolated; it is not without moorings. The Christian's conscience, as Martin Luther saw it, is to be "captive to the Word of God." Scripture does not merely advise or suggest, but as the very Word of God, applied to us by the Holy Spirit, it is our absolute authority.

What does Scripture say, then, about a Christian who disobeys the civil law by intervening on behalf of an unborn child? What are the broad Scriptural principles regarding submission to the civil magistrate? What examples or teaching can be found in the Bible where disobedience to the civil government was approved or even required? Is resistance to abortion an area where the Christian may disobey the law? What guidelines or safeguards should the Christian adhere to if he is civilly disobedient for this purpose?

Debates dealing with the Christian's responsibility to the government, and his obedience to its laws, inevitably begin with a look at two of the more obvious texts on the subject: Romans 13:1-7 and 1 Peter 2:13-17. Both of these passages deal specifically with the issue of submission to the civil authorities. And they are words written under the "acid test" of history; not only were the apostles living under pagan government, but it was the Roman government, a government that held its Caesar to be a god. Christians were subject to persecution, and even death, if that authority were to be seriously rivaled. And yet, even in the face of that kind of relationship to the state, Paul wrote these words to the Christians in Rome:

> Everyone must submit himself to the governing authorities, for there is no authority except that which God has established. The authorities that exist have been established by God. Consequently, he who rebels against the authority is rebelling against what God has instituted, and those who do so will bring judgment on themselves. For rulers hold no terror for those who do right, but for those who do wrong. Do you want to be free from fear of the one in authority? Then do what is right and he will commend you. For he is God's servant to do you good. But if you do wrong, be afraid, for he does not bear the sword for nothing. He is God's servant, an agent of wrath to bring punishment on the wrongdoer. Therefore, it is necessary to submit to the authorities, not only because of possible punishment but also because of conscience.[3]

Examination of this text, and that in 1 Peter 2:13-17, reveals some broad and basic principles:

(1) Civil government is established by God. He made it; it is His institution. It is under God's sovereignty that leaders come to power. Civil government is not an invention of man, nor is it created by man. It is not by nature a "social contract"; it was not born out of a need for authority. God Himself established, and continues to establish, civil governments.

(2) God establishes civil government to promote good and to punish evil. God had a purpose in the establishment of civil government. That purpose was not primarily to put Christians or the Church to the test. The purpose was not extraneous to God's purpose in the plan of salvation; it is not different in kind from His purpose in redemption. The purpose of civil government is to promote (or foster) that which is good, and to punish (or destroy) that which is evil. Civil government is not by its nature opposed to God. Under His sovereignty, it fulfills His purpose, by His own design.

(3) The civil magistrate, in his governing function, is God's servant. The civil magistrate must be viewed as anyone who, by

virtue of his election or his appointment, wields the power of the state. The civil magistrate—whether he be a police officer, a judge, the President, or a Senator—in such an office acts as God's servant. Therefore, he is not first and foremost accountable to the higher courts, his superior in government, or even the electorate. He is (whether or not he is aware of it) God's servant; he is accountable to God.

(4) The Christian must therefore submit to the civil magistrate in his governing function. It is because of the authority that God has given the civil magistrate that the Christian must obey the civil law. In other words, it is precisely because Jesus is Lord that the Christian obeys the judge; that is why he respects and obeys the police officer. As God's servant, the civil magistrate acts for God.

(5) Rebellion against the civil magistrate is rebellion against God and results in God's judgment. When a person disobeys the civil magistrate, he disobeys God; he rebels against God Himself. This is a corollary to the principle that the civil magistrate is God's servant. To the extent that God has delegated His authority in this limited area to a government or official, to that extent when one rebels against the God-instituted authority, he rebels against God. And we are told here, by the Apostle Paul, that God has put teeth in this requirement. If the Christian rebels, there is always the sword of punishment in the hands of the magistrate. The Christian should not be surprised, when he rebels, if he then feels the edge of that sword. For this reason and, more persuasively, for conscience' sake, the Christian is under an obligation to obey the civil magistrate.

In summary: the principle set forth here by the Apostle Paul is that the Christian has a high duty to respect and obey the civil law. But it is of paramount importance to understand why the Christian has such a duty. It is not because government is intrinsically good or right. It is not because the Christian has two separate but equal duties: one to obey God, and one to obey the king. The reason that obedience to the civil law is mandated is that the child of God must obey God. He must obey the One who ordained and instituted civil government. He recognizes that God ordained government, even pagan government, for His glory and for our good.[4]

The Christian's responsibility to submit to or to obey the civil magistrate, like all other "lateral" duties in Scripture, arises out of his duty to obey God. The Bible is full of such lateral obligations, all of which find their roots in our duty to God Himself. Paul commands children to obey their parents "in the Lord"; slaves are to obey their masters out of obedience to Christ; the wife is to submit to her husband as to the Lord; the husband is to love his wife as Christ loves the Church.[5] We pay taxes and we also tithe, not because we answer to two ultimate authorities, but because it is King Jesus who has told us to do both.[6] The Christian has but one Lord; he answers to only one ultimate authority.

It is clear, therefore, that the authority of another human being or institution in any earthly relationship is not intrinsic, and that it is something less than absolute. Absolute authority in any such relationship is human tyranny. Human authority is delegated authority; it does not stand in isolation from the God who instituted it. When Jesus was tried in the Roman governor's court, Pilate asked Him, "Do you refuse to speak to me? Don't you realize I have power either to free you or to crucify you?" But Jesus answered, "You would have no power over me if it were not given to you from above."[7]

Human authority is always conditioned upon, and qualified by, the overarching duty to obey the God who instituted the human authority in the first instance. If obedience to any human authority requires disobedience to God, then a child must disobey his parents, a wife must refuse to submit to her husband, and a servant must disobey his master's orders. A man always stands as a responsible moral agent before his God, whether he is in a position of human authority or under human authority.

Nor can the Christian citizen comply with an order from the government which requires disobedience to God's commands. There are times when the child of God must disobey the law. There are times when God has tested the faith of the believer by challenging him with such a choice. The broad principles of Romans 13 must be read with other Scripture, and Scripture itself reveals numerous incidents where loyalty to God meant disloyalty or even outright disobedience to the earthly king.

The Hebrew midwives, while Israel was in slavery in Egypt, were under clear orders to kill the boy babies being born to Hebrew women. But they knew this was murder; they knew that to obey the king's command would be to disobey their God. They made a choice: they "feared God and did not do what the king of Egypt had told them to do," but saved the babies alive. In fact, they misled King Pharaoh about what they had done: they told him that the Hebrew women were too fast for them—the child was already delivered before they could get to the house to help! For saving the babies' lives, they received not the condemnation of God, but His blessing: ". . . because the midwives feared God, he gave them families of their own."[8]

Likewise, Moses' parents, who violated the same law by hiding their baby from the civil authorities, enjoy distinction in faith's "hall of fame" because "they were not afraid of the king's edict."[9]

Rahab the prostitute was a citizen of Jericho. She lived in a home on the wall of the city. She was under the authority of the city of Jericho; she was under orders from the king of Jericho. When the spies from Israel came to spy out Jericho before Jericho fell to Joshua, Rahab gave them a place to stay. Not only did she house them, but when she found out that the king was after them, she surreptitiously put them on the roof of her house to hide them from the king's men. Then she aided them in their escape. Further, she misled the king about it. She told the king that she had done one thing, when in fact she had done another. She said, "These men took off—I don't know where they went." She pointed her finger in some general direction, and all the king's men charged off. Later, under cover of darkness, she let the Israelites down on the outside of the city wall, so they could make their escape.[10] She was not just disobedient to her civil magistrate; she was a traitor. But how does God regard her for her actions? In Hebrews 11 she is commended because she cared more for the people of God, and for God's rule, than she did for the king of Jericho.[11] Exactly because of her disobedience to the civil magistrate, this many-times great-grandmother of Jesus was spared, along with all her family, from immediate destruction and judgment when the walls of Jericho fell and the city was annihilated.[12]

Ahab and Jezebel, wicked king and queen of Israel during the time of the divided kingdom, issued death warrants for Elijah, prophet of God, and for others among the Lord's prophets as well. A man named Obadiah, who had been given charge of the king's palace, appears on the scene as "a devout believer in the Lord." He made it his business to hide one hundred of the Lord's prophets in two caves and supply them with food and water, to protect them from the king's power.[13]

But the most exhaustive Old Testament pattern for the relationship of the child of God to the civil government is found in the book of Daniel. The accounts found in that book, which records events that occurred while Israel was in captivity in Babylon, give us special guidance in our relationship to the state today. There are significant parallels between the Israelite in Babylon and the Christian in America. Like that ancient empire, America is not a theonomy. As then, non-Christians are in positions of authority in our country; many laws today are largely the product of secular humanism. Like the Israelites in Babylon, Christians are called upon today to support and participate in a secular governmental process. And, like the Israelites, we are commanded (in Romans 13) generally to respect and support the leaders and laws of the land.

To fully appreciate the relationship of the believing Jew to the Babylonian Empire during the Exile, one needs to remember God's words to Israel through Jeremiah. He was God's prophet to Jerusalem preceding the fall of Jerusalem at the hands of Nebuchadnezzar, and at the time of the Exile. As God's prophet to the exiles themselves, Jeremiah commanded the Israelites to obey Nebuchadnezzar, to submit to him, to serve him and not to rebel:

> I gave the same message to Zedekiah king of Judah. I said, "Bow your neck under the yoke of the king of Babylon; serve him and his people, and you will live. Why will you and your people die by the sword, famine and plague with which the Lord has threatened any nation that will not serve the king of Babylon? Do not listen to the words of the prophets who say to you, 'You will never serve the king of Babylon,' for they are prophesying lies to you. 'I have not sent them,' declares the Lord. 'They are prophesying lies in my name. Therefore, I will banish you and you will perish, both you and the prophets who prophesy to you.'"[14]

Jeremiah assured the Israelites time and again that this judgment against Judah was just for a time, and that Nebuchadnezzar was God's servant, His unwitting tool to accomplish a greater purpose. But it was also clear that those who did rebel, and who refused to submit to Nebuchadnezzar, would be punished by the sword. King Zedekiah heard the warnings,[15] but he foolishly rebelled against Nebuchadnezzar and suffered greatly for his disregard for the word of the Lord. When Jerusalem fell, Nebuchadnezzar slaughtered all of Zedekiah's sons before his eyes and then scraped out Zedekiah's eyes, leaving him with the visual memory of that horror until the day of his death in Babylon.[16] God's injunction upon Israel to submit to Nebuchadnezzar, king of Babylon, was not to be taken lightly.

But then the book of Daniel introduces us to three young Jewish men: Shadrach, Meshach, and Abednego. These men were well-educated and would have been fully aware of Jeremiah's commands. They were friends of Daniel, who was highly respected by King Nebuchadnezzar. Things went well for these young Jews until Nebuchadnezzar built a golden image. He set it up in public display, demanding that all his subjects worship the image as a sign of political fidelity. Like Caesar's image on a coin, Nebuchadnezzar's golden image was designed as a symbol of state sovereignty. But these three Jews, who knew that the God of Israel had commanded them not to bow down to any graven image, refused to bow down.

Nebuchadnezzar was furious, but he tried to be fair. He gave them a second chance. He promised them death by fire—his "burning, fiery furnace"—if they disobeyed. The boys did not take time out to do a dissertation on Jeremiah's prophecies; no time for that. Their answer to Nebuchadnezzar was a product of their training. They considered their answer to be the obvious one for those who served the God who held Nebuchadnezzar in the palm of His hand:

"O Nebuchadnezzar, we do not need to defend ourselves before you in this matter. If we are thrown into the blazing furnace, the God we serve is able to save us from it, and he will rescue us from your hand, O king. But even if he does not, we want you to know, O king, that we will not serve your gods or worship the image of gold you have set up."[17]

The *King James Version* translates the first part of their answer as "we are not careful to answer you in this matter." It is not that they were being sloppy, or even disrespectful. They simply meant that they knew that they could not afford to debate the issue. Perhaps they knew the propensity of the human mind and conscience, once engaged in debate, to find loopholes, and they knew, going in, that the issues were clear-cut. They were not willing to risk a violation of God's command.

These men, in fact, stood before two burning, fiery furnaces that day. One was in the present and in full view. But it was temporary and had been constructed by a mortal, temporary king. It was intimidating, but it would exist only a short time. Through the eye of faith, however, they could see another furnace, the furnace of God's judgment against disobedience. Through faith they knew that there would be eternal consequences if they disobeyed a holy God. This is the judgment whereby "the present heavens and earth are reserved for fire, being kept for the day of judgment and destruction of ungodly men."[18] That perception of the reality and the seriousness of God's demands upon them was, in part, what produced their prompt reaction to Nebuchadnezzar. There is a sense in which they were simply making a choice between two furnaces. One held more terror, more permanency, than the other. Since they were looking ahead to a greater judgment than that of Nebuchadnezzar, they made "every effort to be found spotless, blameless and at peace" with God.[19] With this understanding, they really had no choice at all. One thing they did know: they must obey God rather than Nebuchadnezzar.

Their refusal to obey the earthly king resulted in the pronouncement of the death sentence. God miraculously delivered them from physical harm, but that was not the basis on which their decision had been made. Their decision was made because they had wholly committed their allegiance to God, and they left it to Him to deliver them temporally or to let them be martyred; whichever, they would not disobey His commands.

Three chapters and two kings later, their friend Daniel got into trouble. After Nebuchadnezzar's successor Belshazzar had been assassinated by the Medes, Darius the Mede became king. On the advice of Daniel's jealous rivals, that king issued a decree that forbade prayers to anyone except himself for a period of a scant thirty days. Like Nebuchadnezzar's image, this has to be seen as an effort to encourage, or to test, political loyalty.

Daniel conspicuously disobeyed. He went home, threw open the windows, and prayed as normal—three times each day. He intended to be seen and was assured of being arrested, which he was.

He was blatant in his disobedience, and he suffered for it. Like his three friends, he received the death sentence. God again miraculously brought deliverance, this time from a den of starving lions. But Daniel took no chances: he would rather face hungry lions now than a God of judgment later. Like his three friends many years before, he was making every effort to be found spotless, blameless, and at peace with God.

These two illustrations from the book of Daniel place in bold relief the two kinds of life situations in which the child of God is required to disobey civil law. In Shadrach, Meshach, and Abednego's crisis, the king commanded them to perform an act which God had forbidden. On the other hand, the king commanded Daniel to omit an act which God had commanded. These are the two sides of sin: "Sin is any want of conformity unto, or transgression of, the law of God."[20]

It is sin for a man to do that which God has said no to: "Everyone who sins breaks the law; in fact, sin is lawlessness."[21] But it is also sin to fail to do that which God has said yes to: "Anyone, then, who knows the good he ought to do and doesn't do it, sins."[22] Whether the worldly demand is active or passive, God's command is superior and must be obeyed.

The Daniel-Darius crisis, in this regard, is similar to the dispute which Peter and the apostles had with the Sanhedrin in Acts 4 and 5. There, because of the uproar caused by Peter's preaching, the rulers called in Peter and John and "commanded them not to speak or teach at all in the name of Jesus." Peter's first response was: "Judge for yourselves whether it is right in God's sight to obey you rather than God."[23] After being strictly warned, they preached anyway, and they were jailed.[24] The Lord delivered them from jail, and they went back to preaching, fully understanding that they were under legal injunction not to do so. This time, when they were arraigned before the Sanhedrin, Peter did not ask his previous rhetorical question, but replied: "We must obey God rather than men!"[25] Peter and John, like Daniel, could not neglect a positive duty required of them by God, even though the civil magistrate had outlawed their actions.

One of the great conflicts in the earthly ministry of Jesus was His insistence on violating Jewish traditions and man-made laws regarding the Sabbath. Some Christians like to believe that Jesus was very careful to keep all Jewish regulations. But He was not. He fulfilled the law of Moses, the moral Law of God as revealed in the Old Testament. But He did not put up with the law of man where it contradicted the Law of God. The Jewish leaders, through centuries of interpreting and reinterpreting the Mosaic law and honing it to fit their own standards of religion and human behavior, had forgotten the core principle of the law, which was "to love the Lord God with all your heart, and to love your neighbor as yourself." Their human traditions and laws had departed radically from fundamental principles of justice and mercy. Jesus intentionally challenged those regulations. One of the most remarkable such incidents appears in Luke 13:

> On a Sabbath Jesus was teaching in one of the synagogues, and a woman was there who had been crippled by a spirit for eighteen years. She was bent over and could not straighten up at all. When Jesus saw her, he called her forward and said to her, "Woman, you are set free from your infirmity." Then he put his hands on her, and immediately she straightened up and praised God.
>
> Indignant because Jesus had healed on the Sabbath, the synagogue ruler said to the people, "There are six days for work. So come and be healed on those days, not on the Sabbath."[26]

Jewish tradition, embodied in the Talmud, which had the force of law among the Jews, did not permit a doctor to perform the healing arts on the Sabbath except in cases of traumatic injury or emergency. In other words, where there was an organic disease or a long-term illness, the doctor was required to wait until the regular work week to treat the patient, presumably because the patient was not in a life-and-death crisis; in such cases it was considered preferable to wait until tomorrow rather than "break" the Sabbath. That is what the synagogue ruler was referring to. That is one of the reasons that the synagogue ruler was indignant (in addition to his probable jealousy). After all, this woman had been crippled for eighteen years. Twenty-four hours seems like a small price to pay for law and order.

But the Lord could not abide laws that strained out a gnat while swallowing a camel. To imagine twisting the Law of His Heavenly Father to forbid healing, even for a day, to this poor woman! "You hypocrites!" He shouted. "Doesn't each of you on the Sabbath untie his ox or donkey from the stall and lead it out to give it water? Then should not this woman, a daughter of Abraham, whom Satan has kept bound for eighteen long years, be set free on the Sabbath day from what bound her?"[27] In this rebuke, He exposed their ignorance of Old Testament law and their perversion of the underlying principle of justice and mercy. Jesus confronted the civil law, to which the synagogue ruler gave credence, head-on and disobeyed it, because it had been perverted to the extent that instead of advancing the law, it inhibited it.

John Calvin, in his *Institutes of the Christian Religion*, championed the sovereignty of God in government. He clearly set forth the divine institution and support of the civil magistrate, and the Christian's high duty to respect and obey even unworthy or evil rulers. But Calvin never considered that to be an excuse for disobedience to God, or for failure in Christian duty. Whether the ruler is King David or Nero, a command that is issued which is contrary to God's Law is not worthy of obedience. Calvin ends his discussion of the subject of the Christian's duty to the civil magistrate with these words:

> But in the obedience which we have shown to be due to the authority of governors, it is always necessary to make one exception, and that is entitled to our first attention—that it do not seduce us from obedience to him to whose will the desires of all kings ought to be subject, to whose decrees all their commands ought to yield, to whose majesty all their scepters ought to submit. And, indeed, how preposterous it would be for us, with a view to satisfy men, to incur the displeasure of him on whose account we yield obedience to men! The Lord, therefore, is the King of kings; who, when he has opened his sacred mouth, is to be heard alone, above all, for all, and before all; in the next place, we are subject to those men who preside over us, but no otherwise than in him. If they command anything against him, it ought not to have the least attention, nor, in this case, ought we to pay any regard to all that dignity attached to magistrates, to which no injury is done when it is subjected to the unrivaled and supreme power of God. . . .
>
> [A]s if God had resigned his right to mortal men when he made them rulers of mankind, or as if earthly power were diminished by be-

ing subordinated to its author before whom even the principalities of heaven tremble with awe.[28]

In summary: Scripture teaches that the child of God has a high duty to obey the civil law. That duty arises only out of his duty to obey God, who has instituted civil government. Where the civil law requires the Christian to disobey the commands of Scripture, through a sin of commission or omission, the Christian must reject that provision of the civil law. He has no choice but to disobey. He has only one God, only one Person to please. He must obey God rather than men.

How, then, are these Scriptural principles to be applied to the Christian who sits in front of the door of the abortion clinic?

FIVE

CHRISTIAN DUTY AND ABORTION

*M*any Christians have believed that the "safe" place to be is snugly tucked in under the covers of Romans 13. At first glance, this answer seems clear and simple, and so comfortable: Christians simply do not violate the civil law. We pray, we preach, we witness, we may even confront (being careful all the while not to damage our testimony by becoming too disagreeable or judgmental); but Christians are above all else a law-abiding people.

But this dream of easy answers and comfort evaporates when the Christian is awake enough to peer over the bedcovers to look at Shadrach, Meshach, Abednego, Daniel, Peter, and John. Then he discovers that neither Romans 13, nor the rest of Scripture for that matter, was meant to be a place for peaceful slumber. Certainly Christians are to be law-abiding citizens. But man's law cannot be absolutized. Sometimes obedience to a law means disobedience to God. There are times in history when obedience to an evil civil law, or complicity with it, makes the law-abiding citizen a participant in the evil itself, an accessory to injustice.

Is life under *Roe v. Wade* one of those periods of history? Unlike the Shadrach, Meshach, and Abednego crisis, *Roe v. Wade* does not require anyone to have an abortion or to participate in the abortion procedure. Current law does not make the sin of abortion obligatory upon the Christian or anyone else. The state has guaranteed to the citizenry generally the right to abortion, thus making it lawful; but it is strictly a matter of choice—it is required of no one.

How, then, could the Christian possibly justify disobedience to the law at the abortion clinic?

To fairly answer this challenge, it is of paramount importance to understand why the abortion protester typically blocks the doorway. I began to understand this when I viewed the film *Assignment Life*, which was the true story of a female journalist who tracked the abortion story through the clinics and doctors' offices, in what she said was an effort to dispel some of the criticism that was being raised about abortion. The journalist was reportedly "pro-choice" when she began the project, but she ended the project strongly pro-life—all because of some of the facts she witnessed firsthand during her investigative reporting.

There was a scene in that film that made me understand why some people block doors to stop abortion. The movie camera was taken into the "procedure room." A five- to six-month pregnant mother was lying on her back on a draped procedure table, with her abdomen exposed. The abortionist took an oversized needle on the end of a very large syringe which was full of saline solution, and slowly inserted the needle through the abdominal wall into the uterus. The saline solution was then injected into the womb. The narrator described what was taking place, that the salt solution was starving the baby, as it was designed to do, from receiving the oxygen he needed to live. The baby would die within a few hours. In this case, though, it took longer, and the mother felt the baby kicking and struggling for many hours before the baby finally succumbed to the saltwater. After the child's death, labor was induced, and the body of the blackened baby—his skin burned through by the saltwater, and his face twisted in an agonized reflection of what his little body had endured—was displayed on film. I found the scene almost unbearable; I confess that I prefer never to see it again.

When I saw the abortionist getting ready to insert the needle into the mother's abdomen, my reaction (even though I knew I was watching a movie) was immediate and real. I found myself wanting to be there, to pull the syringe out of the doctor's hand, to restrain the man from this murder, to protect the helpless, unsuspecting child. I was not thinking about legal issues or about constitutional rights. I found myself just reacting in a visceral sort of way to the awful injustice that was taking place before my eyes. It was obvious to me that that man had no right to do what he was doing. The baby was innocent and cornered, without a chance. He was locked in his mother's womb, a death sentence upon him, with no one but barbarians (or very confused people) in the room. The baby had no one to stand up for his life, no one to intervene. That is why a man is brought to the point that he blocks a door. It is because of the baby. He attempts to forbid entrance of a pregnant woman to an abortion clinic, even to the extent of violating the law, in order to save the child's life. His purpose in blocking the doorway is not primarily or essentially for publicity, nor to work a change in the law, nor to impose his moral code on the mother or doctor involved—though this is almost always the way he is characterized by the media, and often by other Christians.

These are not his reasons. Rather, he believes it is his duty to do what he can to protect and preserve the life of the unborn child who is only moments away from death. He knows that it is, quite literally, a "do or die" situation. In this way, his action is substantially identical to that of the Hebrew midwives in Exodus 1. He knows that the child is a person and is therefore worthy of protection, even though the Supreme Court refuses to protect the child. He believes that this little person has a right to expect a helping hand in this crisis, and that if he, or someone like him, does not make a fuss, the child will most certainly die.

This "belief" is not a subjective one. It derives from the positive duty implicit in the Sixth Commandment: "Thou shalt not kill." There is, of course, in that commandment the negative prohibition against murder. But there is also a positive duty in the Sixth Commandment: the duty to protect, preserve, and care for our own lives and the lives of our neighbors. It is the duty which Moses summarized as, "Love your neighbor as yourself."[1] This duty, as it is made applicable to the unborn child, is clearly set forth throughout Scripture, but nowhere is the duty more explicit than in this passage:

> Rescue those being led away to death; hold back those staggering toward slaughter. If you say, "But we knew nothing about this," does not he who weighs the heart perceive it? Does not he who guards your life know it? Will he not repay each person according to what he has done?[2]

Christians have a duty to rescue those being led away to death. Christians have an obligation to the helpless on their way to slaughter. A Christian cannot plead ignorance; if he does, the One who guards the Christian's life knows it, and He will "repay" each person according to what he has done (or not done). The focus here is on the one who can help, but who is attempting to avoid his responsibility by claiming ignorance. Like Shadrach, Meshach, and Abednego, the Christian stands in front of two hot furnaces. He needs to make a choice as to whom he fears the most—man or God.

It also must be noted that this duty is not altogether gratuitous; it is motivated by an informed self-interest. Why is it important to rescue those being led away to death? Because the One "who guards your life" is keeping track of what you are doing. He is watching your interest in the plight of others, and the clear implication is this: to the extent that you turn away from the plight of the helpless person on his way to being slaughtered, and just to that extent, your own life is proportionately more at risk. Perhaps this is the principle which the English poet John Donne echoed when he wrote: " . . . any man's death diminishes me, because I am involved in mankind; and therefore never send to know for whom the bell tolls; it tolls for thee."

This principle of Christian duty, of ethical responsibility, is what the Lord taught most comprehensively in the parable of the Good Samaritan in Luke 10:25-37. Unfortunately, the term "good Samaritan" has been diluted in modern usage to refer to one who does something for another person that is, by definition, purely altruistic. But this does not fit the parable at all. Jesus told the story after a Jewish legal expert had asked Him what a person needed to do to inherit eternal life. Jesus responded with a question: "What is written in the Law? How do you read it?"

The expert replied as a good student of the Mosaic law should reply: "'Love the Lord your God with all your heart and with all your soul and with all your strength and with all your mind'; and, 'Love your neighbor as yourself.'"[3] Jesus told him that he had answered correctly. But the expert wanted to "justify himself," so he prodded Jesus with an additional question: "And who is my neighbor?" Jesus told him this story:

A man was going down from Jerusalem to Jericho, when he fell into the hands of robbers. They stripped him of his clothes, beat him and went away, leaving him half dead. A priest happened to be going down the same road, and when he saw the man, he passed by on the other side. So too, a Levite, when he came to the place and saw him, passed by on the other side. But a Samaritan, as he traveled, came where the man was; and when he saw him, he took pity on him. He went to him and bandaged his wounds, pouring on oil and wine. Then he put the man on his own donkey, took him to an inn and took care of him. The next day he took out two silver coins and gave them to the innkeeper. "Look after him," he said, "and when I return, I will reimburse you for any extra expense you may have."[4]

Then Jesus asked the question: "Which of these three do you think was a neighbor to the man who fell into the hands of robbers?" The expert again answered correctly: "The one who had mercy on him." Jesus told him, "Go and do likewise."[5]

It is important to notice here that the entire discussion revolved around the law. It had to do with that which God requires of man, not that which is optional, not that which is extra-credit work. To love the Lord God with all your heart, soul, and mind, and to love your neighbor as yourself, as this Samaritan did, is not a suggestion— it is a commandment. And upon this commandment "hang ... all the Law and the Prophets."[6] This is the heart and soul, the polestar, of the law. This is the core of Christian ethics. To love your neighbor as yourself is to merge self-interest and interest for others into a unified duty. This is the Golden Rule, which was given by the Lord in the Sermon on the Mount: "In everything, do to others what you would have them do to you, for this sums up the Law and the Prophets."[7] We define our ethical responsibility to others not with complex rules of behavior, but by answering, in real-life circumstances, the simple question: "If I were facing the trouble that this person is facing, what would I want others to do for me?"

But what do the parable of the Good Samaritan and the Golden Rule teach with regard to the Christian's responsibilities in the abortion crisis? First, it is important to recognize that the ethical focus is not on the actions of the robbers. Their evil is obvious, but it has little to do with the ethical responsibilities placed upon the priest, the Levite, and the Samaritan. The robbers had beaten this pedestrian and left him helpless in a ditch. Now Christian duty arises. The duty does not run against the criminals. The Christian is not asked to bring the robbers to justice (that may be a separate duty, but it is not the point of the parable). The Christian's duty relates rather to the victim of the injustice, to the man who is helpless, bleeding, and hurt. The Christian is the one who is being judged in this story, not the robbers. When the Christian enters the arena of the neighborhood abortion clinic, the ethical focus is not just (or even primarily) on the doctor who will perform the abortion, nor on the mother who participates in the decision and the killing; the focus is on the Christian's responsibilities to the victim, the unborn child.

Secondly, the parable preaches a duty which arises apart from the known merit or will of the victim. His character, his social standing, his particular importance or quality of life is not known. Nor does the passage reflect that the victim asked for help at all; neither his desire to be helped, nor his ability to ask for assistance, is mentioned. In fact, it is recorded that he was "half dead," indicating that he was in no shape to request aid. The important characteristic of this man is that he is a man who is in desperate trouble; he will die unless someone intervenes. He is in such bad shape that he cannot even request the help he needs.

But thirdly, the passages teach us the measure of Christian duty. What is the Christian's duty to the unborn child at the abortion clinic? "In everything, do to others what you would have them do to you." Do I want to know my duty? Then I must ask what I would want done if someone were about to salt, burn, crush, and kill my body. Would I want that for myself now? Or, if I could turn the clock back to a few months before my birth, would I want to have been born alive, in good health, or to be put to death before I drew my first breath?

I have no doubt what I would want—I would want to live. I would have wanted someone to intervene. I would prefer that someone had taken some extraordinary measures if my life were at stake. I would hope that a doctor would not kill me; but if he were set to do so, I would certainly hope that someone with better sense, and with more concern for me, would stop him.

Is not that the measure of my duty to a child about to be killed by abortion?

At the abortion clinic, it probably will not do much good to rail against the doctor or the evils of abortion, or to condemn this wicked generation. That is, it does no good for the victim, and thus it does not help the Christian in the discharge of his ethical obligations to that victim. Something more is necessary at the abortion clinic.

It is not only the parable of the Good Samaritan, or the Golden Rule, or Proverbs 24 that places this kind of obligation on men. This is the theme, or the summary, of the second table of the law. It was the persistent and increasingly blatant disregard of this duty by the people of God that brought God's wrath upon Israel through the prophets and His ultimate judgment upon the people He had chosen as His own. It was the continued placement of self-interest before the interest of others, or even the serving of self-interest at the direct expense of others, that brought Israel to ruin. This is why God has placed such a premium on the responsibility to defend, protect, and support the innocent, the widow, the weak, and the orphan.[8] This duty could exclude the unborn child only to the extent that the unborn child is excluded from personhood.

Of course, the duty which the Christian has to thus protect and preserve the life of the unborn child is part of the duty to protect the physical well-being (particularly the life) of his neighbor, because the unborn child is his neighbor. The duty to protect others from physical harm, or to insure bodily safety to the citizenry, is really a duty which good government otherwise should undertake through the keeping of the peace.[9] That is one of the principal duties of government, and it is recognized as one of the foundational principles of government in the United States Constitution— "to . . . establish justice, insure domestic tranquility. . . ." Significantly, Paul's discussion of civil government in Romans 13, which is so often raised by Christians as being opposed to any form of civil disobedience, is all within the greater context of his discussion of love (Romans 12:9-21 and 13:8-10). Paul closes the discussion of government with these words: "Love does no harm to its neighbor. Therefore love is the fulfillment of the law."[10] Civil government, which is established by God, is meant by Him to work in generally the same direction as the law of love: by protecting the helpless, by securing legal relief for the oppressed, by establishing justice and insuring domestic tranquility. God-ordained civil government is supposed to be an expression of the Golden Rule.

But civil government (like every human relationship) has been damaged and perverted by sin, and often gets turned on its head in this world. Now, in almost every courtroom in America, the person who takes extraordinary means to help save the unborn child from death is punished, and the abortionist and his staff are given the full protection of the law. The civil government in the United States, in this one area of the law, is punishing those who protect helpless innocents from death. When government does this, it is at war with itself and at war with God, having denied the very foundation of law itself.

Assuming, then, that a moral duty exists to protect the unborn child—that is, that the Christian has the same duty to love and protect the unborn's life that he owes to born children or adults—the Christian is not absolved of that duty simply because the civil law tells him that abortion is legal or that he will not be permitted to protect the unborn child's life. The Christian is no more absolved of that duty because of the civil law than Peter was absolved of his duty to preach because of the civil law in Acts 5. There is no way to avoid this responsibility if we really believe in Christian duty today. As John Calvin has said:

> If they command anything against him [God], it ought not to have the least attention, nor, in this case, ought we to pay any regard to all that dignity attached to magistrates, to which no injury is done when it is subjected to the unrivaled and supreme power of God. . . . [A]s if God had resigned his right to mortal men when he made them rulers of mankind, or as if earthly power were diminished by being subordinated to its author before whom even the principalities of heaven tremble with awe. I know what great and present danger awaits this constancy, for kings cannot bear to be disregarded without the greatest indignation; and "the wrath of a king," says Solomon, "is as messengers of death" (Prov. 16:14). But since this edict has been proclaimed by that celestial herald, Peter, "We ought to obey God rather than men," (Acts 5:29)—let us console ourselves with this thought, that we truly perform the obedience which God requires of us when we suffer anything rather than deviate from piety. And that our hearts may not fail us, Paul stimulates us with another consideration—that Christ has redeemed us at the immense price which our redemption cost him, that we may not be submissive to the corrupt desires of men, much less be slaves to their impiety (I Cor. 7:23).[11]

The Christian whose conscience for the unborn has led him to intervene for a child's life at the abortion clinic does not have an easy road, whether his efforts are legal or illegal. It is work that by its very nature goes without much encouragement or expression of thanks. After all, those most directly affected by the multifaceted pro-life effort—the children whose lives are saved—are not able to show their appreciation. And the person who ventures across the line of the law faces criticism and anger from the police, the court system, usually the media, and sometimes even his friends and family.

Christians should not be surprised at this kind of adversity. John Calvin referred to it as a "great and present danger" awaiting those who choose to obey God rather than men. As a lawyer, I have represented many abortion protesters who have been tried for the relatively minor crimes of trespass or contempt of court in their attempts to intervene on behalf of unborn children. I have seen judges red-faced with anger as they shouted out against the protesters. Most judges cannot stand to have their orders intentionally disobeyed, particularly by citizens who profess to be generally law-abiding. Christians who disobey the law in this way can expect to be punished, and it is very possible that they will be punished severely. Few will be there to compliment, to encourage, or to rally support. It can be a lonely, and costly, effort.

But most evangelical Christians seem reluctant to participate not only in activism of the illegal variety, such as trespassing, but in other direct efforts to prevent abortion as well. The pickets are sparsely populated. There are relatively few Christians who are opening their homes to house and care for unwed mothers. Financial support for Christian adoption agencies and crisis pregnancy centers lags. Efforts in court to battle abortion at various levels go almost totally unfunded. Why are so many Christians inactive?

We generally imagine that our attitudes as Christians regarding abortion are basically correct. We may admit to some lack of diligence (after all, we argue, what area of Christian responsibility do we fulfill perfectly?), but we wish we could do more, and so we trust that our intentions will get passing marks. But we should not be misled regarding our own culpability in this matter. Why is it that we shy away from protecting the unborn child, from intervening on behalf at the abortion clinic when he is about to be killed? It is primarily a matter of priorities. Jobs, careers, schooling, reputation, money, even good standing in the church—all of these are at risk. In short, we are paralyzed by a fear of where this kind of "radical" commitment will lead in the future. It is really self-interest—more bluntly called selfishness—that keeps us from the task at hand; our earthly interests come first. Our comforts, careers, money, reputation, schooling—all of that comes first. To help the child, in other words, may "force upon [us] a distressful life and future."[12] We discover that the very attitude of selfishness—the self-centeredness that brings the young woman to decide in favor of killing her baby— that attitude now keeps us from helping the child in his mortal distress.

Selfishness has poisoned all of us; Christians are far from immune. We too often stand right there in spirit with the woman, at the door of the abortion clinic, refusing to stand up for the life of the child, considering his life to be worth less than our freedom and comfort. In this principle of conduct, I find myself in wholehearted agreement with the pregnant woman who wants an abortion. The child must be sacrificed in favor of my career. The basic principle of this age, the "look out for Number One" ethic, which at first led to the sickness of abortion in this country, now thwarts its cure. Dante, in his *Inferno*, spoke of all of us who thus join the ranks of the willfully passive:

> . . . The dismal company
> Whose lives knew neither praise nor infamy;
> Who against God rebelled not, nor to Him
> Were faithful, but to self alone were true. . . .[13]

God, through His Word illuminating His creation, has given the Christian in particular an insight into the reality, or the truth, regarding abortion. The Christian knows that a child, not a piece of tissue, is being destroyed in abortion. Because of this particular knowledge, the Christian is burdened with particular responsibility. For the believer to take this knowledge, repress it in his mind and conscience, and fail to act in accordance with it is, first of all and most obviously, disastrous for the victim of the abortion. That is the external effect. But there is a personal, internal disaster too—the implosion of the Christian's integrity. We Christians are uniquely aware of the personhood of the unborn, of his life-and-death predicament; but we treacherously turn away from the plight of the child to trim our lawns, plan our vacations, and attend our church outings at the ballpark.

Our inaction on abortion is because of an internal hindrance rather than an external one. But once this hindrance has been identified, by God's grace it can be overcome. Christians can, by the power of the Holy Spirit, answer a call to an increased level of commitment. God's people have risen to the occasion in the past by responding to evils that in many ways were parallel to the abortion crisis. We can learn from, and be encouraged by, their history. We need not find our eternal repose among Dante's "dismal company."

HISTORICAL PRECEDENT: THE UNDERGROUND RAILROAD

*I*magine that you are a Christian living one hundred and forty years ago in the free State of Ohio, just across the river from Kentucky, a slave state. One day you are awakened just before dawn by a knock at the door. It is a poor black woman and her children, fleeing their Kentucky slave owner, hoping to make it north to Canada—to freedom. She requests only lodging for the daylight hours, since she plans to be on her way after dark that night. The only way she can hope to make it to Canada undetected is by traveling at night, and the only way she can do that is with help from people like you during the day.

Of course, you feel pity and a sense of compassion for the woman and her children standing outside your door, waiting for you to answer. You wish you could help them. But you also realize that to house her family, or to assist her in any other way in her mission, will make you a lawbreaker. That is why the family hopes to get to Canada, because although Ohio and all the other northern states are "free states," a federal law enacted by Congress in 1793 provides for the return of black slaves who escape their owners. This law is effective in all states, the northern as well as the southern.

The 1793 congressional act was known as the first Fugitive Slave Law. It made it a crime to aid or abet any slave who was attempting to flee his master. It authorized any federal judge, or any state magistrate, to decide without jury trial the status of a fugitive; and if you harbored the slave, or helped to prevent his arrest, you were subjected to a fine of five hundred dollars.[1] This law was aimed at protecting the "property rights" of the slave owner.

But many considered it to be their duty before God to aid the slave in his escape to freedom, flatly disobeying the law that forbade them from doing so. They would open their doors to the fleeing slave, and many slaves in fact were reaching their freedom. The 1793 law was not doing its job. The slave owners complained loudly that their property rights were being violated. The entire southern economy, they claimed, was in jeopardy, and more effective federal legislation was needed.

In response, the 1850 Congress passed a "compromise" measure which greatly strengthened the 1793 act. This second Fugitive Slave Law provided for stiffer penalties: any person hindering the slave owner from capturing the fugitive, or attempting his rescue or concealment, was liable to a fine of one thousand dollars, imprisonment of up to six months, and civil damages to the "injured" slave owner in the sum of one thousand dollars for each fugitive. There were specially appointed commissioners to aid the federal and territorial judges in bringing the abolitionist activists to justice. Fugitives were not permitted to testify in their own behalf, even though a simple sworn statement by the slave owner would suffice for proof of ownership. As in the 1793 law, the fugitive was denied the right to trial by jury. And as mentioned previously, a fee of ten dollars was paid to the commissioner if he found in favor of the slave owner, and only five dollars if he found in favor of the fugitive.[2]

These laws of 1793 and 1850, the Fugitive Slave Laws, were what forced the abolitionists to go underground. Assisting fugitive slaves on their way to free soil in Canada required a willingness to break federal law. If these illegal efforts were to be at all effective, there would have to be a network of ready, willing, and able lawbreakers who would conspire together to provide safe passage to the slaves. They would have to know secret routes and homes, contingency plans, passwords—all at great risk. This endeavor, which grew in intensity during the seventy years from 1793 through the first year of the Civil War, came to be known as the Underground Railroad. Many, many Christians were involved. Through the Railroad, tens of thousands of slaves were freed. Those who assisted blacks on their road to freedom in those pre-Civil War days risked a great deal. They risked their estates, their reputations, and their personal freedom.

What moved them to such action? Why were they willing to risk so much?

Levi Coffin was one such person. Born in 1798, he ultimately came to be known as the "president" of the Underground Railroad—a distinction which he claimed was conferred upon him by the unhappy slave owners who bitterly blamed him as the moving force behind the secretive efforts to help fugitives to freedom. From 1827 through 1860, Levi Coffin assisted thousands of blacks to safety.[3]

What motivated a man like Coffin to do what he did? Why was he willing to become a lawbreaker for a period of time spanning a third of a century on behalf of others? Primarily it was because he was deeply motivated by a personal understanding of the plight of the slave. He had seen—firsthand—the oppression and torture of black men, women, and children, until his conscience tortured him to do something about it. When he was a young man, still living at home in North Carolina, he saw a black man, a fugitive, snared by his owner in a blacksmith shop where young Coffin was waiting to get some work done for his father. While the frightened slave was being shackled with a neck-ring and handcuffs, his master asked him why he had tried to run away. His slave told him, "My wife and children were taken away from me, massa, and I think as much of them as you do of yours, or any white man does of his. Their massa tried to buy me too, but you would not sell me, so when I saw them go away, I followed." His owner insisted that the black man tell him who had given him his pass to leave the plantation, and when his slave refused, he punished him:

> Laying the slave's fettered hand on the blacksmith's anvil, the master struck it with a hammer until the blood settled under the finger nails. The negro winced under each cruel blow, but said not a word. *As I stood by and watched this scene, my heart swelled with indignation, and I longed to rescue the slave and punish the master.* I was not converted to peace principles then, and I felt like fighting for the slave. One end of the chain, riveted to the negro's neck, was made fast to the axle of his master's buggy, then the master sprang in and drove off at a sweeping trot, compelling the slave to run at full speed or fall and be dragged by his neck. I watched them till they disappeared in the distance, and as long as I could see them, the slave was running.[4]
> (emphasis added)

Levi Coffin resolved to do what he could to right such injustice. In 1826, when he was twenty-eight years old, he settled in Wayne County, Indiana, right on the line of the Underground Railroad. The young Quaker began to participate immediately in covert operations to help free the slaves as they came north into Indiana. He and his wife opened their home to more than one hundred slaves every year, for thirty-three years.[5] All of the Coffins' actions in doing so were blatantly illegal.

Another of the most notorious activists in this work was Thomas Garrett, born in Pennsylvania in 1789. When he was eighteen, a black woman who was employed by his father was kidnapped. Young Garrett succeeded in finding her and freeing her, and from that time on made such "rescues" his life calling. From 1822 forward, for forty years he made direct efforts to aid the fugitive slaves his chief business, all in violation of the Fugitive Slave Laws. One open violation of the law, in 1848, netted him a criminal conviction and bankrupting fines:

> He was tried on four counts before Judge Taney, and his entire property was swallowed up in fines amounting to eight thousand dollars. There is a tradition that the presiding judge admonished Garrett to take his loss as a lesson and in the future to desist from breaking the laws; whereupon the aged Quaker stoutly replied: "Judge, thou hast not left me a dollar, but I wish to say to thee, and to all in this court-room, that if any one knows of a fugitive who wants a shelter and a friend, send him to Thomas Garrett and he will befriend him."[6]

Though over sixty years of age, Garrett was able, with the help of some of his friends, to get enough money together to make a new start. But he claimed disappointment that he had never finished what he set out to accomplish: "The war came a little too soon for my business. I wanted to help off three thousand slaves. I had only got up to twenty-seven hundred!"[7]

Garrett and Coffin were, without question, some of the most active in this kind of civil disobedience, but there were thousands of Christians during the first sixty years of the nineteenth century that were involved in the same effort. Vigorous participants in the work were Harriet Tubman, who executed rescues from her home base in Philadelphia, and Owen Lovejoy, a four-term member of the U. S.

House of Representatives and brother of martyred Elijah P. Lovejoy, who opened his home in Princeton, Illinois, to fugitive slaves. John Rankin, a Presbyterian pastor, moved from his Kentucky pastorate to Ripley, Ohio, in 1821 and for forty-four years opened his hilltop home as a refuge to fleeing slaves. Members of Covenanter Presbyterian congregations in that area of Ohio regularly allowed their homes to be used as stations on the Underground Railroad. And Joseph White, a railroad worker in Western Pennsylvania, reflected that all the men with whom he worked in underground enterprises were Presbyterians.[8] Two Unitarian clergymen, Samuel May of Connecticut and Theodore Parker of Boston, were also committed to open assistance to the fugitives in violation of the Fugitive Slave Laws.[9] Charles Beecher, an eloquent preacher and brother of Harriet Beecher Stowe who authored *Uncle Tom's Cabin*, strongly supported the Underground Railroad from his pulpit.[10] The list of individuals goes on and on.

Institutions also became involved. The principal Illinois stronghold for the "Road" was Galesburg, where the Presbyterians and Congregationalists had established a college in 1837. But southern Ohio probably boasted the most noteworthy institution—Oberlin College, operated by the Congregationalists. By 1835, this college was known as a "hotbed" of abolitionism. It became a notorious station on the Underground Railroad, and because of its reputation for this form of lawlessness, there were four (all unsuccessful) attempts by the legislature of Ohio to yank the school's charter. The school survived.

While the Fugitive Slave Law of 1850 was aimed at cracking down on abolitionists to protect the "rights" of the slave owners, its real effect was to increase the determination of abolitionist Christians to resist the enforcement of the law, which they considered to be contrary to the Law of God. In spite of the severe penalties which it imposed against those who shielded or rescued the refugees from slavery, sympathy for slaves persistently increased. Public meetings were held by abolitionists to proclaim defiance of the law and to inspire those not yet involved to help protect the fugitives.[11] Abolitionists unashamedly called out for increased civil disobedience in rescuing fleeing slaves.

Although he did not publicly address the issue of the Underground Railroad as such, Abraham Lincoln did recognize the insanity of the Fugitive Slave Laws:

It is a very strange thing, and not solvable by any moral law that I know of, that if a man loses his horse, the whole country will turn out to help hang the thief; but if a man but a shade or two darker than I am is himself stolen, the very same crowd will hang the one who aids in restoring him to liberty. Such are the inconsistencies of slavery, where a horse is more sacred than a man; and . . . if one man chooses to make a slave of another, no third man shall be allowed to object.[12]

Were these laws worthy of obedience? Levi Coffin did not think so. He believed that to obey the Fugitive Slave Laws was to disobey God. When he was called before an Ohio grand jury to answer allegations that he had intentionally violated the law by harboring groups of fugitives, he defended his actions:

L– B– then asked me if I understood the statute in regard to harboring fugitive slaves. I told him that I had read it, but did not know whether I understood it or not. I suggested that he turn to it and read it, which he did. I told him that I knew of no violation of that statute in our neighborhood. Persons often traveled our way and stopped at our house who said they were slaves, but I knew nothing about it from their statements, for our law did not presume that such people could tell the truth. This made a laugh among the jury, with the exception of L– B–. I went on to say that a few weeks before a company of seventeen fugitives had stopped at my house, hungry and destitute, two of them suffering from wounds inflicted by pursuers who claimed them as slaves, but I had no legal evidence that they were slaves; nothing but their own statements, and the law of our State did not admit colored evidence. I had read in the Bible when I was a boy that it was right to feed the hungry and clothe the naked, and to minister to those who had fallen among thieves and were wounded, but that no distinction in regard to color was mentioned in the Good Book, so in accordance with its teachings I had received these fugitives and cared for them. I then asked:

"Was I right, Friend B–, in doing so?"

He hesitated and seemed at a loss how to reply. I continued:

"How does thy Bible read? Was it not as I have said?"

"Yes," he answered, "it reads somehow so."[13]

How can a law that punishes a man specifically because he obeys the Golden Rule be worthy of his obedience? These laws punished the

Good Samaritans of Ohio, Iowa, Illinois, Indiana, Pennsylvania, New York, Massachusetts, and other states for doing for the Negro slave—the fugitive from bondage—what one would want done for himself. The question should be posed another way: did the Fugitive Slave Laws deliver the Christian from his duty to "love his neighbor as himself"? Did these laws negate his responsibility to be the Good Samaritan? When the black family knocked at the door, was the Christian not faced with the critical choice that had faced Daniel before Darius? Was it not really just a choice between obedience to God or obedience to man?

Certainly this kind of "radical" obedience to the mandates of Scripture was effective in that it directly produced the freedom of many slaves and their families. But the effect of the Underground Railroad is to be seen in another equally significant way: it constantly, and with an increasingly painful tempo, made a public caricature of the injustice of slavery itself in the minds and consciences of the citizens. In this peaceful violation of the Fugitive Slave Laws, the barbarism and injustices of slavery became more obvious. How? Because it was becoming clear that it was necessary to prosecute, fine, and jail respected citizens—abolitionists—in order to sustain slavery as an institution. The Good Samaritans of the nation were through their simple but courageous efforts forging a solidarity with the fugitives. Those who by their actions helped the slave to freedom were being compelled, because of the act of mercy, to share in the slave's bondage.

But to do otherwise was to them inconceivable. Inaction on the matter of the fugitives meant the continued bondage of black men, women, and children in great sections of the country. But that was not all. Inaction also meant bondage of the individual's conscience. It was not so much that slavery itself was burdening the consciences of the northern abolitionists. Slavery was not universal in the country. But the toleration of slavery was universal. And it was the national toleration of slavery, and indeed its universal advancement and protection by federal laws, that weighted down their consciences. The toleration of slavery, like a chain around a dog's neck, was slowly choking the conscience of the entire country. But as these few brave citizens patiently and persistently showed *de facto* solidarity with the slave, the conscience of the nation gradually became energized.

The evil of slavery became intolerable because of the proximity of slavery itself to the lives and consciences of the citizenry. This proximity of victim to liberator, of injustice to justice, was not brought about so much through books and articles. It was brought about by those who in fact stood in to help the fugitive slaves, and thus the issue was raised, and thus the issue demanded resolution. By acting on the command, "Thou shalt love thy neighbor as thyself," in disobedience to a federal law which commanded the individual to "return your neighbor to slavery and bondage," the injustices of slavery itself came into focus for the nation.

> We can see, at this distance, how clearly slavery was doomed to destruction, from the time the two sections first made it an issue in 1820; but there was no relation arising out of slavery except the territorial question which did so much as the fugitive slave controversy to hasten the downfall of the system. The contrast between the free principles of democratic government and human bondage was forced upon the attention of the North by the pursuit of fugitives in their midst. Yet without national machinery for the recapture of runaways the institution could not have long been maintained. There is no evidence that the North was profoundly stirred by the horrors of slavery before 1850; it was only when the North was called upon, in the Territories, and through the Fugitive Slave Law, to give positive aid to the system that the anti-slavery movement grew strong. Fugitive slaves and fugitive slave laws helped to destroy slavery.[14]

The parallels between slavery in the nineteenth century and abortion in the twentieth century are uncomfortably manifest. John C. Willke, a Cincinnati physician and for many years the head of the National Right to Life Committee, has nicely summarized some of the more poignant of these likenesses in his book *Abortion and Slavery*.[15] Both required a Supreme Court decision: the 1857 *Dred Scott* case ruled that blacks were not persons worthy of protection under the Constitution; the 1973 *Roe v. Wade* case ruled that unborn children were not persons worthy of protection under the Constitution. The slave was considered the property of his owner; the unborn child is considered the property of his mother. The slave owner had the right of choice over the slave—to buy, sell, and in some cases to kill. The mother has the right to choose to keep or to kill her unborn child. Pro-slavery proponents argued vehemently that they did not want to impose slavery on any other states or sections of the country; they only wanted the rights of those that chose to own slaves protected; they objected strongly to the imposition of the moral values of the abolitionists upon them. Pro-abortionists argue that pro-lifers have no right to impose their morality on the mother. And of course the most obvious parallel is this: slavery received, and abortion receives, the full protection of the law.

Or does it? It is true that slavery received the "protection" of the Fugitive Slave Laws and the *Dred Scott* decision, but this protection proved to be relatively short-lived. This "law," it was later proved, was diametrically opposed to the principles of the Declaration of Independence and to the spirit of the Constitution. These foundational principles of the American dream were made of steel; the laws that promoted and protected slavery were shown to be made of paper. Lewis Lehrman has observed:

> I suggest not merely that the issues of slavery and abortion are historically analogous. Rather I say that they are, in a crucial sense, the same issue. Both are but particular cases of the recurring challenge to the first principles of the American Revolution, which forbid the violation of the God-given rights of any person, no matter how convenient such a violation might be for some powerful individual or faction, or even a majority.[16]

It is true, of course, that by the calendar we are about a century and a quarter removed from slavery. Prior to 1973, we may have imagined that America was safely removed from that kind of barbarism. Enter abortion-on-demand.

Happily, the executive branch of the federal government has treated abortion essentially as Lincoln treated slavery more than a century ago in the Emancipation Proclamation. President Ronald Reagan, in January 1988, signed Proclamation 5761, in which he declared that the unborn child was to be protected, as a person, to the full extent of the law.[17] This Proclamation makes a positive finding that the unborn are persons, and that the life of a human being begins at conception. Congress has not spoken. The Supreme Court, in *Roe v. Wade*, did not make a finding that a human being's life did not begin at conception, but simply removed constitutional protection from the unborn child, without coming to a conclusion regarding the life issue. Hence, only one branch of government has spoken clearly on the subject, and the finding is solidly on the side of the unborn. But the courts of America have given the Proclamation no weight; for the most part, judges make themselves beholden only to the Supreme Court on the issue of abortion.

The battle for human justice in America, which has often been considered a world showcase for human rights, is in fact as long as our history as a nation. The historical context is new and ever-changing; the principles and the real parties to the conflict are always old friends and old foes. Yet, the stakes in the present quarrel are greater than in the conflict over slavery, as momentous as those issues were. The atrocities are more pervasive and more extreme than in the darkest days of slavery. In abortion, it is always a life-and-death issue. In abortion, the victim is always trapped and has not grown enough even to have legs long or strong enough to let him try to escape. In abortion, it is not the slave owner who separates a mother from her child; it is the mother herself who kills her child, and who separates herself permanently from the little one who needs her love and care. In abortion, the atrocities are protected in every state. And in sheer numbers, abortion has taken more than twenty-three million lives already.

How does the person who blocks the door at an abortion clinic, attempting to rescue a baby from death, differ from Levi Coffin? Are not both responding to the same Biblical mandate to "love your neighbor as yourself"? Are not the inconsistencies of abortion exactly the inconsistencies of slavery, where, as Lincoln said, "if one man chooses to make a slave of another, no third man shall be allowed to object"? Does not Christian love demand that meaningful objections be raised? If a civil law forbids an effective expression of that love, whether in 1850 or 1989, should the Christian obey that law? Or is obedience to such a law, in reality, disobedience to God?

HISTORICAL PRECEDENT: LE CHAMBON

*F*rance toppled relatively gracefully into Hitler's hand at the beginning stages of World War II. Poland had already been de-
feated on the eastern front in late 1939, and Norway, Denmark, the
Netherlands, and Belgium fell to the Nazi war machine by early May
1940. On the evening of May 12, 1940, the first contingent of
German troops entered French territory. By June 14 Hitler's armies
reached Paris, and on June 16—only thirty-five days after Germany
had entered France—the French government surrendered, requesting
an armistice, the terms of which were enjoined by the Third Reich.
The armistice became effective on June 25. France was now at Germany's mercy and found herself under the direct command of the
Nazi dictator Adolf Hitler.

Doubtless, many of those in positions of authority in France in
1940, having witnessed the quick devastation which German *blitz-
krieg* could produce, were motivated to reach an agreement with
Germany simply out of a concern for self-preservation. France
seemed certain to fall to Germany with or without a fight. But
whatever the reasons, the existing cabinet of France resigned, and a
new "collaborationist" government, under French General Marshal
Pétain, was installed at Vichy. For more than four years France's
puppet Vichy regime would follow and enforce the Nazi agenda for
Europe and for the world. This agenda included the destruction of
the Jews.

It is not quite accurate to say that the spirit of anti-Semitism
was imposed upon France, for much of France had been infected

with that malady long before the German invasion in May 1940. The Vichy regime, under Pétain, in many instances seemed to show more enthusiasm for a program for removal of the Jews from France than did the Nazis, at least in the early stages of the German occupation.[1] It is not clear that those in France who were determined to take care of the "Jewish problem" in their country were at all in favor of the destruction of the Jews, as were the Nazis; but it is clear that they favored doing whatever it took to see that the Jews were removed from France. The ultimate result was that during the course of the occupation, more than seventy-five thousand Jews were deported from France, most to concentration and death camps in Germany and other points east. After the war, less than twenty-five hundred of those deported returned alive. Pétain's Vichy government was the instrumentality through which the roundups of the Jews, and their deportations, were carried out.

So it was that from June 1940 on through the end of the war, Jewish men, women, and children were on the wanted list in France. Early on, it may be that the citizenry did not know specifically what would happen to the Jews after deportation, for the German promise was (among other tales) that they were being taken to a new Jewish colony being established in Poland, where they could live in peace. But very soon it became known that their destination was Auschwitz, Treblinka, and other death and concentration camps. When the knock came at the door, the Jew—and the Jew's neighbors—knew that it meant captivity, suffering, and death at the hands of the Nazi regime. Every Jew became a fugitive.

A fugitive needs help if he is to make a successful escape to freedom. To provide help to the Jew, to harbor the Jew, or to assist the Jew in any way in his flight to freedom in Switzerland, for example, was to disobey the Vichy government. Not only was such care for the Jews disobedience to existing law, but it was obviously a great personal risk to those who assisted them, or who failed to turn a Jew in to the Vichy authorities when his identity and whereabouts became known. To aid the Jewish refugee—actively or passively—in Vichy France, was to violate the civil law in the most egregious way:

> In unoccupied France, overt sympathy toward Jews involved marginal risks at the very beginning of the regime, but a year later such action could mean the loss of one's job, arrest, or far worse. In the Occupied

Zone, Admiral Bard, the Paris prefect of police, posted a decree in December 1941 forbidding Jews in the department of the Seine from spending the night outside their homes, and forbidding anyone from taking them in, "under pain of the gravest penalties." By the summer of 1942 assisting Jews in any way was extremely dangerous in either zone.[2]

Yet there were those few brave souls who risked bringing down the wrath of the Nazi machine on their heads. They housed Jews, hid them from the Vichy police squads, and helped get them out of the country. They considered such efforts to be necessary, their duty to God, regardless of what the law said. Their efforts in this regard were identical in principle to the abolitionists working in the Underground Railroad, and in fact the network of those involved in Europe during the German occupation became known as an underground railroad as well.[3]

One of the most remarkable clandestine efforts to save Jews was undertaken by a small community in southeastern France. The village was Le Chambon-sur-Lignon, populated then as now by Protestants, staunch descendants of the French Huguenots, a religious community with a long history of civil disobedience. First, there was the early persecution of these loyal followers of John Calvin, including the St. Bartholomew's Day Massacre of 1572. Then, more than a hundred years later when the Edict of Nantes was revoked, it became a crime in France to be a Protestant, and the kings of France used the force and authority of civil law to pressure the Huguenots to "abjure" their Protestantism. This kind of persecution ran intermittently from the French Reformation in the mid-sixteenth century through the French Revolution almost three centuries later. The Huguenots' property, their freedoms, and often their lives had been taken simply because of their stand as children of the Protestant Reformation. And this persecution, this deprivation, was almost always carried out under the sanction of French law.

Such a history can infuse attitudes and values in subsequent generations. That is why André Trocmé, himself a descendant of a long line of Huguenots, found it possible to convince his Presbyterian parish in Le Chambon to undertake what proved to be a five-year project in which his entire constituency participated: to welcome, feed, clothe, house, and transport refugee Jews who were fleeing the Nazis in Europe during World War II.[4] Somehow this humble rural congregation rallied to the cause and worked together in defiance of an unjust civil law; in reality, they conspired against the government to protect those who were being victimized by the law. And they did so in the name of the Christian religion. The Le Chambon story is one in which an entire presbytery came into direct conflict (nonviolent, but a conflict nevertheless) with a state bent on diminishing or destroying human lives.

Their pastor, Andre Trocmé, was born in 1901, studied for the ministry in the United States, and took the charge at Le Chambon in 1934. His wife, Magda, and their four children led an uncomplicated life in the remote village pastorate for the first six years, until the German occupation in 1940. It was in the winter of 1940-41, following the summer armistice and installation of the Vichy regime, that the first knock came at the door. André was tending to his pastoral duties, visiting his parishioners; Magda was home alone. She recalls:

> A German woman knocked at my door. It was in the evening, and she said she was a German Jew, coming from northern France, that she was in danger, and that she had heard that in Le Chambon somebody could help her. Could she come into my house? I said, "Naturally, come in, come in." Lots of snow. She had a little pair of shoes, nothing. . . .[5]

That invitation to cross the threshold was just the beginning. Le Chambon soon acquired a reputation, and dozens, then hundreds, and ultimately thousands of Jewish fugitives sought and found refuge in Le Chambon. Cevanol School, which Trocmé had first opened as a private school for children of the parish in 1938, was greatly expanded to take care of the refugee children as they came to the village. The Trocmés' home was opened to the Jews, but more and more of the members' homes in the presbytery were opened as well, in a kind of countryside network, to handle the demands being placed on the church community.

The demands upon the small congregation were, to some extent, induced by Trocmé himself, who had been in contact with the American Friends Service Committee, a relief group working in France. This group, through its own volunteers and other contacts at French internment camps, had been able to rescue some of the

Jewish children and their mothers from deportation. When they could, they arranged for the transportation of such refugees to Le Chambon. To this extent, Trocmé and his followers actively sought out the fugitives whom they were to help.

The pilgrimage of increasingly desperate Jews to Le Chambon began in 1941 as a trickle and gradually increased in volume through the end of the German occupation. The demands thus placed on the little community were very great. It was necessary to prepare false identity cards (for example, changing the Jewish name "Cohen" to "Colin"), to hide the refugees from Vichy officials, to shuffle them from home to home when house searches were carried out by the police, and to make plans for and often to accompany the fugitives as they made the treacherous trip to the Swiss border, where they could hope to receive full protection. This effort required synchronization of the presbytery's *responsables*, group leaders within the parish, each of whom was assigned to care for and coordinate the resources of church families and homes under his care.

There are numerous examples of heroic aid for the Jews during the nightmare of the Holocaust. What makes Le Chambon unique is that it seems to have been a spontaneous effort of an indigenous church which—at incredible collective risk—lent a hand to those who were in a desperate life-and-death plight. By the time the Allied troops liberated France from Germany's grip in 1945, about twenty-five hundred Jews had been be-friended and transported to freedom by the congregation at Le Chambon.

On numerous occasions Trocmé was ordered by the Vichy officials to divulge the identity and whereabouts of the Jews the police believed he was hiding in his congregation. Trocmé refused. He told the officials that he did not know their names, which was technically true since false identity cards were given to them and Trocmé made it a point not to know their real names. But, he added,

". . . even if I had such a list, I would not pass it on to you. These people have come here seeking aid and protection from the Protestants of this region. I am their pastor, their shepherd. It is not the role of a shepherd to betray the sheep confided to his keeping."[6]

This refusal, in the late Summer of 1942, ultimately led to the arrest and imprisonment of André Trocmé, together with two of his coworkers, Édouard Theis and Roger Darcissac. Incarcerated at a Vichy prison camp, they feared deportation. Their fears were not unreasonable. However, the three were mysteriously released a few days before the rest of the inmates were deported and sent to concentration camps in Poland and salt mines in Silesia, where almost all of them died.[7]

The Christians at Le Chambon without a doubt consistently and intentionally violated the law. But they did not see violation of the Vichy law to be their primary duty. Assisting the desperate Jew was their duty at that particular period of their congregation's history. Violation of the civil law was an unfortunate but necessary corollary to their obedience to the Law of God. Theoretically it would have been better if they had been able to carry out their acts of mercy legally. But if voluntary obedience to the law ultimately meant turning one's back on his neighbor and handing him over to the authorities for torture and execution, then the law had to be resisted.[8]

The Christians at Le Chambon believed that to neglect to answer the door when the fugitive knocked, asking for help, was to sin. The language of Romans 13 helped them know their obligation in the matter: "'Love your neighbor as yourself.' Love does no harm to its neighbor. Therefore love is the fulfillment of the law."[9] The closed door, they believed, does harm. Neglect of neighbor meant active harm to neighbor. Turning a deaf ear to him in his time of need was to sin grievously against him and against God. Thus the door must be opened; help must be given. André Trocmé and Édouard Theis preached this duty weekly to the congregation at Le Chambon, as the members faced the increasing demands being placed upon them by the refugees flocking into the village:

> It was this strenuous, this extraordinary obligation that Theis and Trocmé expressed to the people in the big gray church. The love they preached was not simply adoration; nor was it simply a love of moral purity, of keeping one's own hands clean of evil. It was not a love of private ecstasy or a private retreat from evil. It was an active, dangerous love that brought help to those who needed it most.[10]

Trocmé believed that ethical goodness, according to Scripture, is not a vapid concept. It is not simply a child who is a good example, fitting neatly and quietly and passively into the patterns which other people have laid down for him.[11] The ethic which Christ taught in the parable of the Good Samaritan was one of active involvement, of courage, even at times of heroism. Ethical goodness is not passive. It is to love the Lord your God with all your heart, soul, and mind, and your neighbor as yourself. It is intensely active; it is only as "passive" as would be your efforts to protect yourself.

When a Jewish mother and her children were fleeing for their lives in occupied Europe, the last person in the world they needed to run into was a law-abiding citizen. A citizen who obeyed Vichy law was a citizen who would essentially pronounce the death sentence on them. Like the abolitionists who worked on the Underground Railroad, members of the Le Chambon congregation were faced with an ethical alternative: obedience to the law of Vichy France, or obedience to God. They chose obedience to God.

Does the Le Chambon experience have anything at all to do with abortion in the United States today? Is it relevant?

Obviously there are some differences. The Jewish refugee could usually walk and talk, and thus he could ask for your help. The unborn child cannot walk, talk, or ask for help. He cannot knock at your door. But this is not a material distinction, for as the parable of the Good Samaritan teaches, the ability of the "half dead" victim to ask for help is not what gives rise to Christian duty. The victim is by the side of the road; his presence there, in that condition, is what triggers duty. The unborn child differs not a bit from the Jewish refugee in this regard, except that he is in more desperate straits simply because he cannot walk, run, or ask for help.

But another distinction may be raised. One might argue that Marshal Pétain's Vichy regime, as a puppet government under the power of the Nazis, was not worthy of obedience or respect because the government as a whole was illegitimate; the Nazis had usurped a right that was not theirs, and the laws of an illegitimate government need not be obeyed. André Trocmé and his clan at Le Chambon could resist the laws regarding the Jews simply because the government that enacted those laws was an impostor. It will further be argued that we are in no such state of affairs in the United States today, and that although we may agree that the *Roe v. Wade* decision is very wrong indeed, still the government of our country is by and large a good one and a legitimate one. In such cases, goes the argument, we must obey even those particular laws that we find morally reprehensible. Under such an argument, the choice is to continue to work for change within the system, observing even the evil law, until the structure of government itself is so bad that revolution, the overthrow of the government, becomes necessary. This argument, with respect to the authority of civil government, is an all or nothing proposition.

But the Biblical data would counter that argument. The previously cited examples of civil disobedience to particular laws or regulations were not tied to the overthrow of the government, nor was the legitimacy of the government as government questioned or set aside. Daniel and his three friends continued to support and honor the king during and after their disobedience and punishment. Daniel's first words from the lions' den were, "O king, live forever." The principle seems to be: "Fear God, honor the king."[12] When they were commanded not to preach any longer, the apostles in Acts 4 and 5 did not seek overthrow of the government; they continued to preach and to live within the law in all areas where obedience to the law did not require disobedience to God. In this principle, the Apostle Peter, André Trocmé, and Joan Andrews are in accord.

A third argument could be proffered to attempt to establish a distinction between André Trocmé's Vichy France and Joan Andrews' *Roe v. Wade* America. In Vichy France, the issues were absolutely clear. The mass murder of Jewish men, women, and children was morally wrong by any decent person's standards. There was unanimity among the sane and moral citizenry that this treatment of the Jews was an abomination. The government, under the spell and power of an insane Hitler, had for the moment turned criminal, and, except for a small group of madmen, public opinion in Europe and the world was as outraged as we are today at what proved to be the slaughter of more than seven million people. It is further argued that in *Roe v. Wade* America, the issue is still being debated. For example, the argument goes, neither the American Church nor the American citizenry show unanimity on the abortion issue.

But we too easily assume that the world's present outrage at the Holocaust existed universally—at least in the free world—while the mass slaughter was being carried out. In point of fact much of Europe was indifferent to the plight of the Jews. Many of those who believed that it was wrong nevertheless did not want to become involved in helping the victims of the Holocaust—because of the trouble it would cause to resist the government, because of the high degree of risk. André Trocmé was an exception to the norm. He was one of a small minority of French churchmen who was radical enough to get involved. Trocmé was approached by ecclesiastics in the Reformed Church of France on several occasions, urging him to become a law-abiding citizen and cease his disobedience to the state in his attempts to help the Jews. Jacques, the Trocmés' second of three boys, one evening overheard his father talking with one of the top leaders of the Reformed Church of France, who had come to visit André Trocmé to endeavor to convince him to come back into line:[13]

Leader: What I want to say to you is this: you must stop helping refugees.

Trocmé: Do you realize what you are asking? These people, especially the Jews, are in very great danger. If we do not shelter them or take them across the mountains to Switzerland, they may well die.

Leader: What you are doing is endangering the very existence not only of this village but of the Protestant church of France! You must stop helping them.

Trocmé: If we stop, many of them will starve to death, or die of exposure, or be deported and killed. We cannot stop.

Leader: You must stop. The marshal will take care of them. He will see to it that they are not hurt.

Trocmé: No.

The bottom line for this leader of the Reformed Church of France and the bottom line for the evangelical Church in America today is essentially the same: temporal safety. What Trocmé was doing was dangerous. It involved not only himself, but his congregation, his village. It also held potentially dangerous ramifications for the whole Reformed Church of France, if the Vichy government in any way could determine that Trocmé was acting in a kind of legal agency for the greater Church. (Some parts of the mainstream pro-life movement and the organized Church today criticize those engaging in illegal rescues, claiming that they are "endangering the whole movement." Could it be that they are beginning to fall into the same pattern of thinking?)

Finally, there is the argument that in Vichy France civil disobedience may have been proper because there the government itself was the perpetrator of the wrong. It was the SS and the Vichy police squads acting on behalf of their government leaders that coordinated the roundups of the Jews, their internments, their sorting in cattle pens, their shipment to Germany and Poland, and their mass executions. Not so in the United States today. The government here has permitted the killing of the unborn infant, but the government does not order it, participate in it, or otherwise make abortion a matter of public policy or prescription. The killing of the unborn infant is a choice and an act of the private citizen. Thus, the argument concludes, disobedience to the civil magistrate is not justified, since the civil magistrate is not the protagonist.

But the fallacy in such an argument has to do with the very purpose for which the person who intervenes at the abortion clinic does what he does. His purpose is not to resist government. His purpose is to protect the life of the child who is about to be killed. In other words, if abortions were illegal, and an illegal abortion were about to take place, failing other means the abortion protester would do the same. His moral responsibility does not rise or fall based upon the identity of the perpetrator of the wrong. His duty arises because of his responsibility to the victim, whether the victim's life is threatened by the Nazis or by a private abortionist. As in the story of the Good Samaritan, the identity of the robbers is unimportant.

EIGHT

ACTIVISM, ABORTION, AND ANARCHY

"We will not have anarchy!"

The judge was nearly shouting as he reproved the courtroom full of abortion protesters and their supporters, friends who had sat with them through their trial. It was a picture-perfect Fall day in October1984, but seventeen men and women had just been tried for criminal contempt of court, for trespassing on the private property of a St. Louis abortion clinic. One was acquitted. One was excused by the judge because he promised the judge that he would not go back on the property. Fifteen were convicted and sentenced—all to jail, for terms of from three days for first-timers to five months for recidivists.

The judge had found that these fifteen defendants had intentionally violated his order, which had been clearly posted on the abortion clinic property on the day of the protest. The order notified the public, and particularly the anti-abortion folks, to stay off the property. The defendants had intentionally violated his order; they went on the property, sat in front of the clinic's door, and attempted to forbid entrance to the abortionist doctors and the patients who were seeking their services.

The judge knew that these now-convicted protesters were otherwise good citizens. Like Joe Wall, every one of them had testified to their Christian commitment and general respect for the law in court just before sentencing. They had told the judge that they did what they did out of obedience to Christ and Scripture. Furthermore, they made it clear to the judge that they were not at all sorry for what they had done—that if given the opportunity, their consciences would most certainly take them back to the clinic for another round. To them, it was a matter of conscience, a conscience directed and bounded by the Word of God. The judge's order forbidding their acts could not be obeyed.

A civil court judge does not very often have to deal with a courtroom full of people who are willing to tell him not only that yes, they violated one of his orders, but also that yes, they did so intentionally, and that yes, they would have to do it again if given the chance. Even the most heinous felon (out of fear of penalty, if nothing else) will make a pretense of agreement with the judge as to the court's authority, and will probably deny that he committed a crime, or at least that he did so intentionally. He certainly would profess an intention never to get into trouble again in the future and would promise the judge anything if he could get lighter treatment. But the abortion protester, who has violated an injunction in order to attempt the rescue of an unborn child, is a different kind of animal.

His remorse is not for his disobedience to the judge's order, but only for the state of the law. Obviously if justification for his actions is founded upon his conscience, he could not be expected to promise the court or anyone else that he will agree to violate conscience in the future just to avoid present punishment. His attitude is akin to Thomas Garrett's response to Judge Taney after the judge had convicted him in 1848 for violation of the Fugitive Slave Laws: "If anyone knows of a fugitive who wants a shelter and a friend, send him to Thomas Garrett and he will befriend him."

The judge sees the abortion protesters as "taking the law into their own hands"; or, as Judge Anderson said of Joan Andrews, "She is not bound by the laws that bind others." They do not play by the rules. What these judges fear, and what they mean to avert (as public servants should, generally), is exactly what the St. Louis judge objected to in 1984: anarchy. Webster defines the word as "a state of lawlessness or political disorder due to the absence of governmental authority." Anarchy is lawlessness, where differences are settled not in the halls of justice, but in the streets. The word literally means "apart from rule" or "rulerless." Every decent citizen recognizes the importance of preventing such a state of affairs in our country, or in any part of our country. Christians in particular are enjoined from promoting a spirit of lawlessness in Romans 13 and 1 Peter 2.

The Christian agrees with the principle espoused by the St. Louis judge: "We will not have anarchy." When we take disputes to the street, social disorder and chaos are the immediate consequences. This is true even though the values we may be seeking to protect are high ones and well worth fighting about, because anarchy eclipses particular rights by suspending all rights.

However, it needs to be understood that because of abortion in America today, the country has already been thrust into a state of anarchy. That state of anarchy began on January 22, 1973, and it continues. The very essence of well-ordered society, and especially the essence of the government of the United States of America, is our protection of one another through laws and government. It is particularly essential to government that such protection exist—for everyone—in matters of life and death.

But the Supreme Court, in *Roe v. Wade*, took legal protection away from the unborn child. As far as the child was concerned, his law was now gone. No more "well-ordered society" for him. From January 22, 1973 on, it is every unborn child for himself. The unborn child was rendered "apart from rule" or "rulerless" as far as his protection was concerned. The *Roe v. Wade* Court says something like this to the unborn child: "Little one, from now on, your mother can kill you if she wants to. It's entirely up to her. Before now, our laws and courts protected you, but we are today withdrawing that rule of law. If your mother decides to let you live, then you will be allowed to grow up like the rest of us; but if she decides to kill you—well, that's up to her, not us.

"And if she does decide to kill you, and some friend of yours tries to help you, we're going to have to send out the police right away and arrest your friend and put him in jail. We must have laws, and we must have order. We hope you understand."

Roe v. Wade made anarchy a rule of law. This is not a theoretical point; it is a point of fact. A doctor in a hospital in America today may be delivering a six-month preemie by C-section and making every effort to keep the baby alive, solely because the mother wants the child alive, and may then move to the next room to "deliver" another six-month preemie with the specific intention of putting the baby to death, solely because the mother wants the child dead. The *Roe v. Wade* ruling, in which one class of human beings has been abruptly deprived of protection, has suddenly put all human lives at risk. This is true not just because the Supreme Court assumed to itself the power to make such life-and-death decisions for the rest of us, but because it granted to millions of the citizenry the particular power to kill or to save alive. This is anarchy not in its most sophisticated but in its most primitive form.

Abortion is privatized infanticide. What the Supreme Court really did in 1973 was to deputize every pregnant American woman, giving her the power to make a life-and-death decision regarding another person. Private citizens may now pronounce the death sentence in America for their own private reasons, under the sanction and protection of the law. And private citizens have done so more than twenty-three million times. The highest court of this land has told these citizens that they may do so, and that the decision may be based upon their convenience or their comfort. One out of every three lives in America today is cut down in this form of anarchy.

Roe v. Wade is anarchy in its worst form, first because it has made such lawlessness a rule of law, but secondly, and more crucially, because it allows lives to be taken in unlimited numbers, without any sort of legal process or protection for the victims. By comparison, it is preposterous for a judge to accuse the abortion protester of anarchy when he has made a feeble, nonviolent attempt to rescue a child from death. The Supreme Court is the anarchist. It has thrown the most basic life-and-death issues out on the street, so that every mother may "duke it out" with her unborn child.

It is this anarchy that the rescuer seeks to redress. By his confrontational action, he brings this anarchy into focus. Where true anarchy exists, it should be exposed. It is the nature of proper civil disobedience to highlight, or exemplify, a failure of government qua government:

> Disorder is not injected into society by those who challenge unjust laws, but by those who write and enforce them. When, in a society professing a dedication to justice, unjust laws are maintained, the society is in a state of moral confusion. Those who use whatever means seem necessary to draw attention to the situation do not create the disorder; they simply identify and refuse to cooperate in the disorder which is already there.[1]

It is to be expected that good citizens will be putting up some kind of fuss where an atrocity is being carried out. When part of a healthy body is infected, antibodies rush to the scene. There will be soreness and swelling. There will be, that is, if the body's immune systems are working. We should not be surprised if there is a showdown in front of the abortion clinic. Rather, we should be very concerned about the health of the country if in such a situation good people remain perfectly quiet and well-ordered. But in America, thank God, it is becoming evident that you cannot kill babies without someone trying to stop you.

The Christian who sits in front of the door at the abortion clinic is not there just (or even primarily) to bring attention to the underlying disorder, however. His primary purpose, as mentioned before, is to protect the baby. In this way he goes for the jugular. He attempts to prevent the anarchy itself. By preventing the doctor from putting the forceps, the suction machine, the curette, the saline solution to the baby, to that extent he prevents the discrete anarchic act. The great anarchy which exists in every state in the United States of America today is not caused by trespassing, but by courts that protect and give official sanction to the whimsical slaughter of infants.

It is difficult to distinguish the anarchy existent in the United States today from the anarchy of Idi Amin's Uganda in the early seventies. Kefa Sempangi, a professor and pastor in Kampala, Uganda's capital city, wrote of the daily atrocities during January 1973 in and around Makerere University, where he taught:

> The bodies of Amin's first victims had been buried in mass graves. Later they were thrown into the river or burned with petrol fires. Now, dozens of bodies were simply left to rot, unburied, in the streets of Kampala. Even the thick stone walls of Makerere University could not keep out the dead. More than once I passed mutilated and discarded bodies on my way to the classroom.
>
> One day in January of 1973 I attended a meeting of the university fine arts department to discuss with my colleagues a five-year development plan. The meeting moved slowly and my mind often wandered. I thought of the pressing concerns of the church and I wondered how much longer I could continue to be both a pastor and a professor. They were both full-time jobs, and I seldom had time for my family. Our daughter Damali, now almost a year old, was growing

up without me. With this thought my eyes met the eyes of a fellow professor. He was a brilliant man with a compassionate and friendly face, and I saw that he too felt a deep distraction. He looked away, but a few minutes later he spoke aloud. His voice was flat, as if he were living in a dream.

"It is most strange," he said. "Here we are sitting to discuss a five-year plan and just now on my way to this building I passed five dead bodies."[2]

It is very possible to live in a society where anarchy reigns, and to continue to function, at least on the surface. Sempangi and his fellow-professor passed a few dead bodies on the way to class. They found themselves, just as this was happening, discussing five-year development plans, careers, and child-rearing. It is not that these matters were unimportant, or that they should have been wholly ignored during Amin's reign of terror. But the existence of those more routine concerns was no barometer of whether a truly anarchic state existed.

We should not imagine, just because it seems to be pretty much "business as usual" in America today, that an anarchic state does not exist. There have been more than twenty-three million innocents slaughtered under the protection of our government's laws, judges, and police forces. Sempangi walked by mutilated and discarded bodies on his way to work in the morning. Many Americans—every morning of the week—drive by mutilated and discarded bodies as well, in America's hospitals, clinics, and dumpsters. The only difference is in the size of the bodies.

It is important to keep (or gain, if one doesn't yet have it) perspective on the relative seriousness of the two anarchic acts taking place at the abortion clinic. One man trespasses on another's property, with the motive to save a life. Another man intentionally slaughters a baby, for pay. Is not the former eclipsed by the latter? We are not saying that two wrongs make a right, or that one evil is justified by a greater evil.

This principle, in fact, is recognized in most jurisdictions. It is called the "doctrine of necessity," which constitutes the defense of "justification" in criminal actions brought against citizens for petty offenses. A typical statute setting forth this defense is Missouri's, based on the Model Penal Code:

> . . . [C]onduct which would otherwise constitute any crime other than a class A felony or murder is justifiable and not criminal when it is necessary as an emergency measure to avoid an imminent public or private injury which is about to occur by reason of a situation occasioned or developed through no fault of the actor, and which is of such gravity that, according to ordinary standards of intelligence and morality, the desirability of avoiding the injury outweighs the desirability of avoiding the injury sought to be prevented by the statute defining the crime charged. . . .[3]

Law should, and often does, follow common sense. If a man sees a child leaning out of a second-story window of a burning house, screaming for help, he should not have to answer to a charge of the crime of trespass if he were to run past a "no trespassing" sign, going onto the property to help the child. The desirability of avoiding injury to the child outweighs the desirability of avoiding injury to the property owner through trespass, according to ordinary standards of intelligence and morality. It is not that values are relative. It is rather that, given certain extreme conditions and eventualities, a lesser "harm" is no harm at all.

None of this, of course, ameliorates the disorder that actually exists at the abortion clinic when a group of protesters sits in front of the door. There is no way to soften what is, in fact, taking place. The protesters are defying the law; there is no doubt about that. But we have already come to the conclusion that not all lawlessness is wrong; breaking the law is not intrinsically evil. The reason is simply this: there is a higher law, the Law of God; and the rescuer faces (as do all of us) an uncomfortable dilemma—will he be guilty of anarchy in the kingdom of this world, or will he be guilty of anarchy in the Kingdom of Heaven? It is the same dilemma faced by Daniel, Shadrach, Meshach, and Abednego.

But this kind of "lawlessness" is also something which is soundly American. It was foreseen by our Founding Fathers and expressed in the Declaration of Independence:

> . . . We hold these truths to be self-evident, that all men are created equal, that they are endowed by their Creator with certain unalienable Rights, that among these are *Life*, Liberty and the pursuit of Happiness.—That to secure these rights, Governments are instituted among

Men, deriving their just powers from the consent of the governed.—
That whenever any Form of Government becomes destructive of these
ends, it is the Right of the People to alter or to abolish it. . . .
(emphasis added)

In this foundational document, the essence of rule by law is set forth.
There is a clear recognition of supervening rights or freedoms which
are above any human government or set of laws. These rights define
law and governmental authority; law and governmental authority
never have and never will define or establish these fundamental
rights; they will only recognize them. These rights do not spring
from the law; the law springs from these rights. Certain truths are
"self-evident"; they are not products of a vote or legislative decision.
One of these truths is that human beings have been endowed by their
Creator (not by their government) with unalienable rights—rights
that no man nor any government can cut off or abridge. This
includes the right to life. The very purpose of government is to
secure these rights, to protect them (Romans 13). But when a
government becomes "destructive of these ends," it is the right of the
people to alter or abolish it.

Two observations are in order. One: the men who signed this
document did not envision working "within the law" in the accomplishment of the ends which are set forth in the Declaration of
Independence. The Declaration was directed to the British Crown,
and it was clearly contrary to and defiant of the king's authority
under British law. Those who signed it, and the country of patriots
whom they represented, had to back up their words with force of
arms. The Revolutionary War was the result. When the Declaration
of Independence says that the people have a right to "alter" or
"abolish" government, it is expressly not talking about legal means.
That is the whole point. Legal means have become "destructive of
the ends" of the unalienable rights and by definition must be circum-
vented, opposed, altered.

It is also important to notice that the framers of this document
did not want to leave the citizen with revolution as the only choice.
Some have so argued—that one must put up with evils in government, and obey even bad law, until the government as a whole gets
so oppressive, so impossible, that overthrow of the government itself
is justified. Intermediate acts of disobedience and defiance, the

argument goes, are not merited; it is an all or nothing proposition. Such an argument flies in the face of logic. Is the lesser not included in the greater? Those who drafted the Declaration of Independence recognized the right to "alter" by extralegal means, as well as to "abolish" by extralegal means. Thus, where government becomes destructive of even one of these fundamental rights, which no government may cut off, it becomes the right of the citizen to employ nonlegal means to alter it.[4]

Anarchy (lawlessness) exists whenever the law within the body politic is self-contradictory—or, in a broader sense, whenever the law contradicts the moral Law of God. Law cannot long be at war with itself. A Lutheran clergyman, having just observed two days of a trial of Christians who had violated a court order at an abortion clinic in 1984, told the author that it was obvious that "the law is at war with itself."

So it is. Not only are the foundational principles of individual liberty and right to life contradicted by *Roe v. Wade*, but courts find themselves making increasingly arbitrary rulings in related cases outside the abortion arena. Take, for example, the 1988 case of *United States of America v. Garland Spencer*,[5] decided by the United States Court of Appeals, Ninth Circuit. In that case, Garland Spencer was convicted of murder because he had assaulted Rena Blackgoat, kicking and stabbing her in the abdomen. Rena did not die, but the fetus which she was carrying did die, after premature delivery. Spencer was charged with murder under the United States Code,[6] and the Ninth Circuit upheld the conviction of murder:

> In view of Congress's intent to reflect the state and common-law definition of murder when it passed the statute, and the state and common-law acceptance of infants who died subsequent to birth due to fetal injuries as human beings, it seems clear that Congress intended fetal infanticide to be included within the statutory definition of "murder" under 18 U.S.C. § 1111.[7]

Or take the law which has developed directly from the *Roe v. Wade* decision. In the series of cases since 1973, we see astonishing results flowing from that ruling—astonishing not because they are at all inconsistent with *Roe v. Wade*, but because they so obviously violate long-settled legal principles and standards of moral conduct. A wife can kill her preborn infant without informing her husband, the father of the child, and can abort over his objection if he is informed. A minor can obtain an abortion without informing her parents, though it has long been the law that a doctor should have permission from the parents before treating a minor. In *Thornburgh v. American College of Gynecologists*, in which the 1986 Supreme Court struck down provisions of a Pennsylvania statute intended to control abortion, then Chief Justice Warren Burger (who sided with the majority in *Roe v. Wade*) noted in uncharacteristically agitated language, in his dissent, what a bizarre harvest is being reaped from *Roe*:

> The Court's opinion today is but the most recent indication of the distance traveled since *Roe*. Perhaps the first important road marker was the Court's holding in *Planned Parenthood of Missouri v. Danforth*, 428 U.S. 52 (1976), in which the Court held (over the dissent of Justice White joined by Justice Rehnquist and myself) that the State may not require that minors seeking an abortion first obtain parental consent. Parents, not judges or social workers, have the inherent right and responsibility to advise their children in matters of this sensitivity and consequence. Can one imagine a surgeon performing an amputation or even an appendectomy on a 14-year-old girl without the consent of a parent or guardian except in an emergency situation?
>
> Yet today the Court goes beyond *Danforth* by remanding for further consideration of the provisions of Pennsylvania's statute requiring that a minor seeking an abortion without parental consent petition the appropriate court for authorization. Even if I were to agree that the Constitution requires that the State may not provide that a minor receive parental consent before undergoing an abortion, I would certainly hold that judicial approval may be required. This is in keeping with the longstanding common law principle that courts may function *in loco parentis* when parents are unavailable or neglectful, even though courts are not very satisfactory substitutes when the issue is whether a 12-, 14-, or 16-year-old unmarried girl should have an abortion. In my view, no remand is necessary on this point because the statutory provision in question is constitutional.
>
> In discovering constitutional infirmities in state regulations of abortion that are in accord with our history and tradition, we may have lured judges into "roaming at large in the constitutional field." *Gris-*

wold v. Connecticut, 381 U.S. 479, 502 (1965) (Harlan, J., concurring). The soundness of our holdings must be tested by the decisions that purport to follow them. If *Danforth* and today's holding really mean what they seem to say, I agree we should reexamine *Roe.*[8]

When the Declaration of Independence recognizes the God-bestowed right to life, and modern courts deny that right, it is not surprising that we find the law at war with itself. It is not surprising that cases, statutes, and common law principles will contradict one another. So it was in the days before the Civil War, before the Emancipation Proclamation, before slavery was abolished. The Declaration of Independence was clear in its expression of the principles of human freedom and individual dignity. But the law (some thought even the Constitution) seemed to protect the institution of slavery. Something had to give. Lewis Lehrman, speaking of that conflict over slavery, has made the point eloquently:

> But the insurgent noise would not be silenced. For the muffled murmur throughout the land was the sound of the slave, his tortured breathing rustling the pages of the Declaration of Independence, scaring up from the dry parchment the great truths placed there by Jefferson. For the needs of nation-building, for the sake of a union between slave and free states, slavery may have been legalized in the Constitution. But it was the Creator, as the Founders proclaimed in the Declaration, Who gave men the unalienable right to life and liberty. This contradiction, like a house divided, could not stand.[9]

The Christian who disobeys the law at the abortion clinic today is accused of taking the law into his own hands, of trivializing law and order. He is adjudged to be an anarchist. But it is the Supreme Court that has contravened the Declaration of Independence and the moral Law. The Supreme Court, in this instance, is the anarchist. Those citizens who now, out of fidelity to America's foundational principles and the moral Law, openly resist the Supreme Court at the abortion clinic to protect the lives of the unborn are the true lovers and promoters of the law.

SOLIDARITY WITH THE UNBORN

*T*he unborn child needs help from his friends. He needs someone who will empathize with him, who will identify with his plight, who will adopt the troubles which he faces. The unborn child cannot face his troubles successfully on his own. He needs a companion who will identify with him and do for him what he is utterly unable to do for himself.

But before this kind of help can be expected, there must be a real union of interests between the born and the unborn. There must be what the Polish factory workers, referring to their commonality of interests as set against the Communist regime, have termed "solidarity." *Webster's* defines *solidarity* as "an entire union of interests and responsibilities in a group; community of interests, objectives, or standards."[1]

Solidarity with the unborn means at least two things: (1) full recognition of the unborn child's full membership in the human race, and (2) full treatment of the unborn child as a member of the human community in fulfillment of his essential interests as a human being. Such recognition and treatment are not severable. One cannot meaningfully recognize the personhood of the unborn child unless he treats him as a person. Solidarity means a complete union of interests and responsibilities, and to verbalize recognition without consonant treatment is to demonstrate no union of interests at all. Joan Andrews has written:

The closer we are to the preborn children, the more closely identified
are we with them; the more faithful we are, we become more identi-
cally aligned with them. This is our aim. This is our goal: to wipe out
the line of distinction between the preborn discriminated against and
their born friends, becoming discriminated against ourselves; incur-
ring the wrath and enmity of the anti-child societal forces. Good!
This is necessary. Why should we be treated differently?

The closer we are aligned with the preborn, the stronger the bond,
the more we will be discriminated against, persecuted, rejected. The
rougher it gets for us, the more we can rejoice that we are succeeding;
no longer are we being treated so much as the privileged born but as
the discriminated against preborn. And the gap narrows between born
and preborn, as between "whole" and handicapped. We must become
aligned with them completely and totally or else the double standard
separating the preborn from the rest of humanity will never be elimi-
nated. I don't want to be treated any differently from my brother, my
sister. You reject him, you reject me![2]

Solidarity with the unborn can be demonstrated in a variety of ways.
During the July1988 Democratic National Convention, 134 pro-
lifers were arrested in Operation Rescue in Atlanta. These individuals had blocked the doors of abortion clinics, claiming that their
actions were necessary to save the lives of particular unborn babies
about to be killed at the clinic. When they refused to move, they
were arrested, jailed, and charged with criminal trespass. The protesters refused to give the police their names when arrested, identifying themselves only as "Baby Jane Doe" or "Baby John Doe."
Their anonymity was not intended as a gimmick, but was an attempt
to identify more fully with the unnamed unborn. By refusing to give
authorities their names, these Atlanta rescuers recognized that they
would continue to be held in jail pending trial, because they understandably could not be released on bond without identification and
addresses. But in this forfeiture of personal rights, they participated
in the anonymity of the unborn who, for lack of proper identity and
recognition, had lost an incalculably higher right than freedom from
jail: the right to live.

Such an identification of interests with the helpless can, for the
Christian, be a powerful illustration of the solidaric relationship between Christ and the sinner, and is in turn a witness to that greater

truth. Man, in his sinful state, is helpless—destined for certain judgment and death. He is utterly "without hope and without God in the world."[3] Like an unborn child, man is not only unable to save himself, but in himself, in his natural state, is totally unaware of the disaster that awaits him if he is not saved. Destruction is certain unless someone who is able to help empathizes, identifies, and intervenes. Jesus voluntarily became "like his brothers in every way,"[4] and fully identified with the interests of helpless sinners (whose interest it is to be saved from sin and death) and made their interest His own. During His days on earth, Jesus voluntarily made Himself weak and vulnerable, and He "offered up prayers and petitions with loud cries and tears to the one who could save him from death."[5] Having fully identified with helpless man, He cried out to God for His own deliverance from death, thus incorporating in His personal victory over death all of those whom He was unashamed to call His brethren. This is solidarity par excellence.

The parable of the Good Samaritan, more fully discussed in Chapter Five, has at its heart the solidaric relationship between the helpless victim and the Samaritan. That parable defines what it means to be a neighbor; true neighborliness really is solidarity. But it is not just a human relationship that is taught; the parable is meant to illustrate much, much more than the need for the Red Cross. The Samaritan's action is significant because it demonstrates God's mercy expressed to the world in Christ. The Samaritan is "good" because he is a living witness, a real-life example of saving grace. That is why his actions are so significant. The Samaritan was a "little Christ" who testified through his actions to the reality of God's love for helpless man.

Solidarity with the unborn necessarily means action for the unborn. The Good Samaritan, but for his actions, would not have been good but bad. Solidarity therefore requires that which was discussed in Chapter Two: moral integrity.

The wise man, Scripture tells us, built his house upon a rock. The foolish man built his upon the sand. Perhaps because of the familiar chorus which has set that parable to music, which most of us learned as children, we might assume that the rock and the sand are what distinguished the two. Most Christians do not remember that the Lord, when He introduced these two characters, said that "everyone who hears these words of mine and puts them into practice is like a wise man who built his house on the rock." But "everyone who hears these words of mine and does not put them into practice is like a foolish man who built his house on sand."[6] There is only one thing that differentiates the wise man from the foolish man, and that is integrity before God. Putting God's truth into action is the line of demarcation between wisdom and foolishness. It is not words, but obedient action that makes the difference between a house that stands firm and one that disintegrates when the storm comes.

Scripture is filled with passages where God places His primacy on actions instead of words. One such example is found in what God said to Ezekiel:

> As for you, son of man, your countrymen are talking together about you by the walls and at the doors of the houses, saying to each other, "Come and hear the message that has come from the Lord." My people come to you, as they usually do, and sit before you to listen to your words, but they do not put them into practice. With their mouths they express devotion, but their hearts are greedy for unjust gain. Indeed, to them you are nothing more than one who sings love songs with a beautiful voice and plays an instrument well, for they hear your words but do not put them into practice. When all this comes true—and it surely will—then they will know that a prophet has been among them.[7]

In 1988, those of us in the pews as well as those behind the pulpits are justly rebuked by this passage. We twentieth-century Christians seem to be principally interested in words. In our man-made formulae defining what it means to be "a believer," we have largely reduced the whole business to words. We believe that we begin the work of evangelism if we make the invitation to "come and hear the message that has come from the Lord." We believe that we have successfully completed the work of evangelism if we can extract the right code words from the person we are evangelizing. We speak and we listen to words, words, words. But we do not put many of them into practice ourselves, nor do we communicate God's demands for action to those whom we evangelize. The words of our religion are becoming little more than catchy tunes; we are captured by the aesthetics of the oratory, but it often does neither us nor the world any good, because we do not apply what we have heard.

The fact of abortion in our generation, though it is ind abomination, directly challenges this hollowness of words in the Church. The mass killing of the unborn demands a response beyond talk. Thus abortion unmasks false religion. We love to believe that the evil surrounding abortion is outside the Church, and fail to understand that God is permitting the evil to abound for a time to sift and to judge the visible Church. Harold O. J. Brown has said:

> On a number of occasions, I have argued that the present United States policy on abortion represents a "perfect" challenge to America's Christians—perfect because it is complete. It confronts us at almost every level of our being as Christians and as citizens, and it is the most intense challenge that can be expected short of persecution of the church. It is perfect in this sense too, in that Christians are challenged on principle in abortion, not with respect to their persons, and the church is challenged with respect to its integrity, not with respect to its immediate survival. Of course, we may well believe that the long-term survival of the church, indeed its very claim to be the church of Jesus Christ, cannot be separated from the integrity with which it deals with particular problems. Nevertheless, abortion is not—as taxing might be—a direct life-threat to the church. It is "only" a threat to the integrity and fidelity of the church, to what Paul calls "the whole counsel of God" (Acts 20:27). We write "only" advisedly, because it seems evident that failure of the church to maintain a consistent and coherent pattern of biblical life and thought across the whole spectrum of its life and testimony quickly undermines any claim to be God's edifice and makes it little more than what Karl Barth referred to as a pious club of those interested in salvation.[8]

It is revealing that when the typical evangelical pastor preaches about abortion today, sixteen years after *Roe v. Wade*, it is usually an attempt, once again, to convince the listener that the unborn child is a person. The question is, as always, "When does life begin?" It is a tired attempt to convince us on a Biblical basis (usually with supporting medical facts) of that which we already profess. But our pastors and preachers generally steer clear of any discussion as to what burden we might have as Christians, or what effective steps we might take to protect these children from death. The result of such preaching is that the parishioner feels increasingly helpless and frustrated. Preaching that stops short of practical application is always so, and it produces spiritual death in the Church, because faith without works is dead.

There is admittedly one bit of application which the pastor will usually give. That is that it is the Church's fault in the first place, for not caring for—in fact, for ostracizing—the unwed mother. If we had not been so pharisaical, so judgmental, she would have felt accepted and would have gone to our adoption agency rather than to the abortion clinic. We are told that we must open our doors to those with unwanted pregnancies. We must involve ourselves with them; we must show them the love of Christ.

All of this we need to hear. Most Christians have failed indeed to provide real help, to show meaningful shepherding and hospitality to the young woman who does not believe that she can bear and nurture the baby she is carrying. Certainly it is possible that God has permitted abortion itself in part to expose the inaction and failures of the Church in this regard.

At the same time, we recognize that Christian duty is being fulfilled by many Christians every day in efforts to help the unwed mother and her child: the establishment of telephone hotlines, crisis pregnancy centers, counseling programs, adoption agencies, shepherding homes, and all the rest. Many such efforts have been greatly augmented by Christians since 1973. These actions are born out of a love for Christ and neighbor, and they form a significant part of the aid package that the unborn child desperately needs.

But despite all these efforts, there is still that unborn child today who is being taken into the abortion clinic to be killed. The business of killing goes on and on. Do we show real solidarity with the unborn child if our determination to help him ends short of intervention at the clinic? Important as our duties of love and care for the mother are, and as causally connected to abortion as our failures in these duties might be, this bleak fact remains: babies will still be slaughtered during the next week, and during the weeks, months, and years after that unless their lives are defended. Citing again the parable of the Good Samaritan, the ethical duty which arose was toward that particular victim. Prison ministries to those who left him half-dead, and social rehabilitation or educational programs to prevent such atrocities in the future are duties indeed;

but they do not help the half-dead victim lying in the ditch by the side of the road.

We would like to believe that the 1989 victim—the unborn child—will be helped in his plight by someone's signature on some dotted line. Perhaps it will be by a new judge or two being appointed to the Supreme Court; perhaps by an act of Congress; perhaps by a constitutional amendment. Certainly we hope and pray that such changes in law will occur. But we need to realistically assess what the future holds, even if, say, *Roe v. Wade* is reversed. What will then have been accomplished? Will the unborn child be protected?

In short, no. All that *Roe v. Wade* did was to rule the laws of the several states to be unconstitutional, insofar as those laws prohibited abortion. A reversal now would throw the issue back to the states, for each of them to determine on their own to what extent abortion should be regulated or prohibited. A reversal would not accomplish what a Human Life Amendment to the Constitution would do, which would be to extend constitutional protection for the unborn, mandatorily, upon all the states.

If *Roe* is reversed, we can safely assume that some states—with now more than sixteen years of abortion experience behind them—would pass legislation legalizing abortion, at least to a level that would be intolerable to pro-life Christians. New York, for example, had legalized abortion-on-demand three years before *Roe v. Wade* was decided. Would it not be reasonable to expect other states to enact laws legalizing abortion? One thing seems clear: even if the United States Supreme Court reverses itself, fifty separate legislative battles (and subsequent judicial battles in both state and federal courts) are almost certain to erupt. Pro-lifers will find themselves engaged in fifty arenas of combat. And a new states' rights conservatism on the high court, which understandably would arise out of the same conservatism which generated a particular justice's anti-abortion bent, could work counter to pro-life efforts in the courts to protect the life of the unborn in states like New York, where pro-abortion laws are on the books.

We certainly should pray that *Roe v. Wade* will be reversed. But we should not expect that the battle would thereby be won, nor should we expect or hope that no demands will be made of us in accomplishment of the goal. We are often too much like those inactive citizens described by Thoreau: "They hesitate, and they regret, and sometimes they petition; but they do nothing in earnest and with effect. They will wait, well disposed, for others to remedy the evil, that they may no longer have it to regret."[9]

The battle will not be won effortlessly. History is full of records of nations and peoples whose liberation from captivity, slavery, or even genocide has been won, where their futures have been secured. But how many of these moral battles have been won on paper? Does history contain any record of triumph over genocide which was effected merely by the stroke of a pen? Certainly the emancipation of the American slave did not occur simply because it suddenly dawned on the law that someone had made a mistake. Abraham Lincoln, in his Second Inaugural Address, given on March 4, 1865, before the end of the Civil War, reflected on the judgment of God upon the nation and the awful price which was then being paid for the freedom of the slave:

> The Almighty has his own purposes. "Woe unto the world because of offenses! for it must needs be that offenses come; but woe to that man by whom the offense cometh." If we shall suppose that American slavery is one of those offenses which, in the providence of God, must needs come, but which, having continued through his appointed time, he now wills to remove, and that he gives to both North and South this terrible war, as the woe due to those by whom the offense came, shall we discern therein any departure from those divine attributes which the believers in a living God always ascribe to him? Fondly do we hope—fervently do we pray—that this mighty scourge of war may speedily pass away. Yet, if God wills that it continue until all the wealth piled by the bondman's two hundred and fifty years of unrequited toil shall be sunk, and until every drop of blood drawn with the lash shall be paid by another drawn with the sword, as was said three thousand years ago, so still it must be said, "The judgments of the Lord are true and righteous altogether."[10]

We beguile ourselves if we imagine that the rights, the freedom, the personhood of the unborn child will someday be quietly agreed to by the Supreme Court or by the Congress or by a Constitutional Convention. It will not be so simple. The right of the unborn child to life protected by our laws will have to be purchased, and the purchase price has not yet been paid. Solidarity with anyone headed for slaughter naturally figures to be a costly business. We do ourselves no favor and we do the unborn no good if we fail to count the cost.

To some extent we understand our objective, at least from a legal standpoint. It is to have a firm definition of life, so that the unborn child, from the moment of conception on, has the legal status of a born human being. We want this definition of life, and of personhood, to be a solid and permanent one—not one that depends upon momentary majorities in Congress or the Supreme Court, nor for that matter on the popular whim of the electorate. We need to have the life of the unborn defined and protected, and this needs to be permanent.

But life for the unborn will never be durably defined in Washington until it is first defined at the door of the abortion clinic. Law follows fact more than fact follows law. If I cannot defend a child's life at the moment of the child's death, I cannot convincingly defend the child's life in the courts, in the legislature, or in the pulpit. My failure to show solidarity with the child in real life puts the lie to my oral arguments. Whether we like it or not, life is being defined every day of the week at the doors of America's abortion clinics, and the definition is a photocopy of *Roe v. Wade*. The abortionists by their actions, and most of us by our inaction, treat the unborn as nonpersons. Thus, *de facto*, we are defining the unborn child out of the human race. We are writing the laws of the future by our failures at the door of the clinic.

None of this is meant to discount the importance of making every effort to get anti-abortion legislation through state legislatures and Congress, or of continuing to argue every case involving abortion in the courts in an effort to get the law changed, or of pursuing multitudes of other remedies in the public forum. We must constantly be working at all levels and be using every means available to gain protection for the unborn through the law. But those endeavors will prove flimsy, ineffective, and transient unless they are undergirded by solid efforts to protect the individual lives of the unborn infants at the place and time of their intended murders.

COMMITMENT TO ACTION

W hat must we do? How shall we begin to put what we profess and believe about the unborn child into action? And where do we draw lines?

First, let it be understood that Christians, in the arena of the current battle on abortion, cannot advocate the violation of the civil law per se. The Christian's goal is not to break the law, contrary to the objective in some traditional forms of civil disobedience. The objective is to rescue the child. Every available legal means should be sought in attempting to meet this objective.

It is obvious that there are many things to do. We need to be diligent in finding out where political candidates stand on abortion, and get those elected that not only "personally" are opposed to abortion but who have by their public statements and votes proved their pro-life stance. We need constantly to be bringing this subject to the minds of fellow-believers in the Christian community and challenging one another to action. We need to support organizations such as the Christian Action Council, which has set up a national network of crisis pregnancy centers so that women in distress can call in to get counseling and be given the means and the direction to seek answers other than abortion. We need to support our Christian adoption agencies, and many of us need to let such agencies know that we would be willing to act as "shepherding homes" for unwed mothers, or (in some states) to open our homes as foster homes for newborns waiting for the court to approve their adoption to their new parents—a difficult but joyful way to lend a hand. There is great need in each of these areas of opportunity to show the love of Christ, and many babies have been saved and will continue to be saved through these efforts.

But more is needed. We cannot ignore the children about to be slaughtered at the abortion clinic.

It is essential that we think of the local abortion clinic realistically; we should take it for what it really is. It is a slaughterhouse. It is a death camp. As Christians, we should recognize the need to encircle the local abortion clinic—both figuratively and literally—to stand between the baby and his assailant, to do whatever we reasonably can do to stop the murder from being carried out.

Christians need to provide a circle of protection for the unborn child. This circle of protection can be viewed as having multiple concentric rings around the moment of the child's death at the hands of the abortionist. The largest circle, the most distant geographically and temporally, includes the efforts of writing, speaking, campaigning, and voting, all of which are efforts to turn public opinion against abortion. Inside that ring are the provision of hotlines and crisis pregnancy centers and adoption services, where the objective is not so much to affect public opinion generally as to affect the opinion of the mother, the individual who will be making the abortion decision. Further inside are legal pickets and sidewalk counselors, who attempt to shift the mother's opinion at the last minute before the abortion is to take place.

As the circles get smaller and tighter, they focus increasingly on the unborn child as an individual who is about to be killed. As the child is brought toward the doors of the clinic, more and more direct means are necessary if his life is to be preserved. The pro-life effort must become more proximate, both in time and space, as the moment of the murder of the child approaches. ChristyAnne Collins, Joan Andrews, Joe Wall, Ann O'Brien, and Randy Terry's Operation Rescue in Atlanta constitute the smallest circle—the most direct approach, the most individually oriented.

All of the means, from the largest circle to the smallest, are linked as part of a defensive battle plan to accomplish this ultimate goal, which is to save the unborn baby from death. All of the means employed in the large circles—writing, speaking, campaigning, and voting—are obviously legal, as are all of the positive efforts within the greater Christian community to provide for the unwed mother: adoption and related matters. Some of the more direct approaches, such as pickets and sidewalk counseling, are legal activities and have proven to be very effective in some areas. If the picketers and counselors stay away from blocking the doorways to the abortion clinic, and if they do not trespass on the abortion clinic's property, there is usually no violation of the law. And where legal pickets are large enough, it is possible to force an abortion clinic to close its doors to business because of the general congestion in the area.

Participation in a picket at an abortion clinic during its regular business hours helps one to visualize the circles of protection, and thus is an important exercise for anyone who calls himself pro-life. The dynamics of the issue become clearer at the abortion clinic— when the abortionist doctor is seen striding into his clinic, when pregnant mothers come in cars (often being driven there by their boyfriends or mothers). The woman seeking the abortion is often upset, perhaps crying, often seeming uncertain of what she is about to do. The boyfriend or the girl's mother are the ones most likely to be angry at the picketers, and the ones most interested in keeping the woman's mind set on getting the abortion. They know, and if you are observing you know, that within a matter of minutes the disposal of what is to them a problem, and what is to you a child, will be a *fait accompli*—that if they can just get into the abortion clinic, into the hands of the abortionist doctor and his staff of counselors, their "problem" will be solved for good. What you have known about abortion in theory now becomes a visible fact—a fact that is not very comforting: a human being will be killed, virtually within your presence, within the next few minutes.

The typical picket at an abortion clinic almost always includes direct efforts to contact the mother, to get her to change her mind. The signs that the picketers carry are intended to do just that. Some picketers will call out to the pregnant woman, warning her of what an abortion really is, of what devastation it will work on her if she proceeds with her plans. Sidewalk counselors are even more specific and direct. The pleading goes on, in one form or another, until the mother gets up to the door of the clinic.

But when the woman gets to the door of the abortion clinic, the full weight of moral duty is felt by the onlooker: what should be done if all the means of persuasion have failed?[1] From the point of view of the individual child who is about to lose his life, should not some further action be taken? Here is where the rubber meets the road.

Mere talk is no longer adequate for that particular child. When all efforts at changing the law, at shifting public opinion, even at counseling the mother who is contemplating abortion, have failed, attention must turn solely to the child who will be the victim if the intended course of action is carried out.

Consider again the child as he is brought to the door of the abortion clinic. While *Roe v. Wade* is the law of the land, the last thing in the world that the unborn child needs at that point in time is a law-abiding citizen. The law says that no one can interfere in the killing, but interference at the door of the abortion clinic is the only hope the child has. At that moment, meaningful protection of the child will mean violation of a law, exactly as meaningful protection of Jews in 1943 Europe and slaves in 1843 United States required violation of the law. It is not that the objective is to violate the law. The objective is to protect the unborn child, and violation of the law becomes necessary to meet that objective.

This "final step," this crossing of a line that is done with such fear and trepidation, and which is criticized and condemned outright by so many Christians, is an act which lends credibility to everything else which we are saying and doing in the pro-life movement. It is thus of great importance that those who seek to save the lives of the unborn through legal means not ostracize those who block the door. Those activists at the door of the clinic help to ratify all that we intend to do for and say about the unborn child. For if at the moment of decision for the child we shrink from his physical protection, and from those who are at that instant attempting to provide it, we negate by our actions what we have been proclaiming with our mouths.

The rescuer who sits in front of the door at the abortion clinic, or who enters the procedure rooms or other offices of the establishment to stop abortions from occurring, is doing something quite different in kind from that which has been done up to that point in each of the larger circles of defense. Up to that point we have been treating abortion as *Roe v. Wade* has said we must treat it: as a matter of free choice for the woman. Every effort prior to the woman's walking through the door of the clinic has been aimed at convincing her against abortion. Even the legal picketers and sidewalk counselors in fact treat it as her choice, which is precisely what *Roe v. Wade* said that it was. These efforts to convince the woman against abortion are essential, and must be not only continued but increased at every level. But if those who concentrate their efforts in this sphere of activity turn their backs on those at the door of the clinic, the credibility of their urgings to the pregnant woman will be badly damaged.

The man or woman who sits in front of the door says, for the first time, "No. I cannot allow this murder to take place. It is not that I want to deny you your rights. It is because another human being is about to be killed. You are about to kill that person. I must intervene on his behalf, regardless of your choice." In so doing, he speaks authentically of the non-negotiable humanity of the individual child whom the mother is carrying in to be killed. It could be argued that the rescuer is the one who really treats the unborn child as a person. Stopping short of some kind of intervention at the door of the clinic, or failing to support those who do intervene, is to abandon the child at the most critical point. By his act of intervention, the rescuer is doing what cannot be done adequately with a thousand speeches or books on the subject: he is defining the unborn child as a person in fact.

That is not to say that the work in the outer circles is of no value, or even of less value, than that done on the inner circles. There are virtually unlimited tasks to be performed in the battle for the unborn. Some of the best practical suggestions have been compiled and published in a paperback book by Joseph Scheidler, a long-time pro-life activist from Chicago.[2] Only one chapter in the book is devoted to illegal "sit-ins"—demonstrating perhaps the great number of legal methods of resistance to abortion which can be undertaken. What each person decides to do, and whether or not he personally chooses to violate the law, is of course a matter that will be determined by an individual's conscience and circumstance. Those battling for the unborn should be seen as an army: some will be in the front lines of the battle; many more will be strategically situated as support troops, well back of the front lines.

But just as it is essential for each of us to demonstrate solidarity with the unborn, so it is essential for us to demonstrate solidarity with each other. If those who confine their efforts to the outer circles speak and act against those who attempt actual rescues of the unborn child, their credibility begins to disintegrate. When one speaks or acts against the rescue efforts of the person intervening at the abortion clinic, he is defining the unborn child as something other than a person. The rescuers, as we have said before, ratify the work of others.

If, on the other hand, protesters sitting in jail snub less dramatic efforts as second-rate (something which the author, by the way, has never seen happen), then another kind of damage will be done. That is because people operating in the wider circles are needed to define and legitimize what people on the inside circles are doing as well—to answer in a concrete way, for example, the persistent and unfair complaint by outsiders that door-sitters would be better off, say, arranging adoptions. Of course, people such as ChristyAnne Collins who travel in more than one circle are perhaps the communications "glue" of the pro-life movement.

Many more people and much more time, money, and expertise are needed in all spheres of activity in the battle against abortion. It is not essential (nor is it realistic to expect) that every pro-lifer block a door, but it is essential that the pro-life movement give these rescuers their support financially and spiritually. It is also important that each Christian consider personally how best to show real solidarity with the unborn. Many more bodies are needed in front of the doors. For the sake of the children, the doors to America's abortion clinics must be plugged tight. The attempt to do so is monstrously difficult and discouraging when only a dozen or so participate. When hundreds are involved, as in 1988 (when there were sixteen hundred arrests in New York during one week, four hundred in Philadelphia, and more than two hundred in Atlanta in Operation Rescue), the work becomes less demanding on the few. Sheer numbers make a great difference.

Christians have a direct responsibility to close the doors of the abortion clinics, and while their participation is a matter of conscience, it is a conscience guided and directed by the Word of God. The Christian's conscience is one whose priorities are set, not subjectively, but through an objective understanding of Scriptural demands. It is a conscience that is aware of God's eye upon men, and more particularly of God's eye upon the individual Christian. God has placed a want ad for spiritual and moral courage in societies such as ours where injustices such as abortion are not just tolerated but promoted. There have always been very few applicants:

The people of the land practice extortion and commit robbery; they oppress the poor and needy and mistreat the alien, denying them justice. I looked for a man among them who would build up the wall and stand before me in the gap on behalf of the land so I would not have to destroy it, but I found none. So I will pour out my wrath on them and consume them with my fiery anger, bringing down on their own heads all they have done, declares the Sovereign Lord.[3]

There are only a handful of those who are willing to "stand in the gap," to throw themselves into the breach at America's abortion clinics. Because there are so few, their personal risk is proportionately much greater than it would be if many more Christians involved themselves to the same extent. The jails of this country, crowded as they may be, are hardly being filled to capacity by Christians who have gone to bat for the unborn.

Men and women are needed who have the spirit of Shadrach, Meshach, and Abednego—not a crowd of rambunctious rebels, fueled by the freedom of a self-styled religious zeal in showing open disrespect for the civil law. Those who believe that God has appointed them to impose Old Testament law on every creature in God's creation, making a kind of "citizen's arrest" on those who break God's Law, should probably not participate. The proud, the superior, the morally self-righteous will likely not endure the pressure. The Christian who disobeys the law at the abortion clinic must maintain an unpretentious, meek spirit with respect to the law. He should have a generally high respect for the civil law and the magistrate who attempts to enforce it (even though the magistrate may be wrong in doing so). While acts of disobedience may be necessary to fulfill Christian duty, the Christian citizen must recognize that not all government or all law is therefore to be disobeyed, disrespected, or demeaned. The attitude to be cultivated is one of firmness, of humility, of unswerving resignation to the demands of Christ. But it is also an attitude of "O King, live forever!" when the Christian is being lifted out of the lions' den.

Nor should the Christian who participates in this activity be primarily interested in publicity. The media will often be there. The Christian may be on the local TV news that night. But his goal should be more to care for an unborn child and for simple obedience to Christ than media attention.

The Christian who so violates the law in his attempt to rescue the unborn child should also remember that many fellow-Christians will fervently disagree. The decision to step over the line, to disobey the law within the confines of this particular issue, almost always energizes anger and strong expressions of disagreement from some of the Christian's closest family members and friends.

Part of this may be that the conscience is being pricked. Sometimes a close Christian friend goes further than I go in his "commitment." I may sense that he is essentially right, but if I feel that I cannot or will not make the same degree of commitment, I may tend to resent that friend. The tendency is to frame arguments against radical plans, sometimes out of a genuine concern for the welfare of the person who is "turning radical," sometimes because of conscience. This kind of reaction is common among committed Christians who are closest to the activist who decides to cross the line. But we need to give more room to one another. I need to prayerfully support the friend who wishes to be obedient in this "drastic" way and, while honestly examining my own conscience, recognize that his action need not serve as the standard for my sphere of involvement.

Whatever the reason for the disagreement and friction which are sure to develop, the activist must remember where he once was himself on this issue. Not all Christians will be where he is at a given point in time. Uncertainty and ambiguity always seem to surround acts of civil disobedience within the greater Christian community today. The Christian activist must act with humility, out of a sense of duty rather than superiority, and should refrain from harsh judgment of brothers and sisters in the Lord who are not ready to take the same step.

Most importantly, the Christian who stands in direct opposition to abortion by placing his own body between the body of the baby and the abortionist, in an effort to save the baby, needs to remember the spiritual nature of the battle. It is not primarily a political, a social, or even a moral battle, "for our struggle is not against flesh and blood, but against the rulers, against the authorities, against the powers of this dark world and against the spiritual forces of evil in the heavenly realms."[4] We will not win the battle against abortion, or any other battle, in the power of the flesh. Acts of courage at the abortion clinic will yield no lasting fruit—either for the child who is immediately at risk or for the cause against abortion in general—if those actions are not undertaken in total dependence upon the power of the Holy Spirit, and if they are not grounded in prayer.

The foes who face us in the battle for the lives of the unborn are intimidating. We would easily be overwhelmed if left to our own strength. But we are not left to our own strength. We have infinite resources of power, wisdom, and strength to wage this war when we act with obedient integrity in demonstrating love to the unborn child, and when we look to God in prayer for help as we do so.

But we commit a fatal error if we consider the theater of this war to be primarily external. The soil upon which this battle must be fought is the soil of my own heart. Am I willing to act with integrity toward the unborn child? Am I willing to obey God's commands, though it means disobeying the commands of men? Do I recognize that like Shadrach, Meshach, and Abednego I stand between two fiery furnaces—one erected by mortal Nebuchadnezzar, and one the eternal fire of God's judgment? Am I truly committed to obedience to God at all costs? Or is my profession of faith in Him and my fealty to His Lordship just so much talk?

What are our reasons for noninvolvement? Why are Christian counseling centers so underfunded and understaffed? Why is there so little fuss at the clinic—so few picketers (perfectly legal), so few sidewalk counselors (perfectly legal), so few lawyers to represent the rescuers (perfectly legal)? Why are our pastors so lethargic on the subject? Why are there so few willing to block doors and passageways? Maybe we fear for our families—that we will be in jail, unable to support them, unable to be good parents (and certainly we would not want people abandoning their own children in this effort). Perhaps we fear for our jobs and careers. We fear for our reputations within and without the Christian community. We fear we may be "going off the deep end," and that we will live to regret being swept into a fringe group.

Yet, do we put jobs, careers, reputation, physical security, and all the rest above our responsibility to obey God? Even as I think of my family, would I rather have my children and grandchildren say of me that I was so committed to obeying God that I was willing to go

to jail, or that I was so committed to my career that it took prece-
dence over God's commands? What kind of heritage do I want to
leave my children?

It is time for those of us who are Christians, in this matter of
the unborn, to take to heart the sound exhortation of J. I. Packer:

> We are unlike the Christians of New Testament times. Our approach
> to life is conventional and static; theirs was not. The thought of
> "safety first" was not a drag on their enterprise as it is on ours. By
> being exuberant, unconventional, and uninhibited in living by the
> gospel they turned their world upside down, but you could not accuse
> us twentieth-century Christians of doing anything like that. Why are
> we so different? Why, compared with them, do we appear as no more
> than half-way Christians? Whence comes the nervous, dithery, take-
> no-risks mood that mars so much of our discipleship? Why are we not
> free enough from fear and anxiety to allow ourselves to go full stretch
> in following Christ? . . . One reason it seems is that in our heart of
> hearts we are afraid of the consequences of going the whole way into
> the Christian life. We shrink from accepting burdens of responsibility
> for others because we fear we should not have strength to bear them.
> We shrink from accepting a way of life in which we forfeit material
> security because we are afraid of being left stranded. . . . We shrink
> from breaking with social conventions in order to serve Christ be-
> cause we fear that if we did, the established structure of our life would
> collapse all round us, leaving us without a footing anywhere. It is
> these half-conscious fears, this dread of insecurity, rather than any
> deliberate refusal to face the cost of following Christ, which make us
> hold back. We feel that the risks of out-and-out discipleship are too
> great for us to take. In other words, we are not persuaded of the
> adequacy of God to provide for all the needs of those who launch out
> wholeheartedly on to the deep sea of unconventional living in obedi-
> ence to the call of Christ. Therefore, we feel obliged to break the first
> commandment just a little, by withdrawing a certain amount of our
> time and energy from serving God in order to serve mammon. This,
> at bottom, seems to be what is wrong with us. We are afraid to go all
> the way in accepting the authority of God, because of our secret
> uncertainty as to His adequacy to look after us if we do.
>
> Now let us call a spade a spade. The name of the game we are
> playing is unbelief. . . .[5]

ELEVEN

THE ETHICAL
MANDATE AND GRACE

Studying Christian ethical responsibility can be intensely discouraging. It is easier to outline the standards, to quote the Scripture, to show the radical demand than it is to work it all out in real life. The parable of the Good Samaritan, the illustration par excellence of the Christian's ethical responsibility discussed in Chapter Five of this book, may not be all that comforting to most of us. The conclusion that my responsibility to the unborn child is to do for him what I would have done for myself—if I take it seriously—is tough to swallow. It would not be so difficult if we adopted the worldly exegesis of that parable, that the "charitable duty" taught in the story is not really a requirement at all, but good for earning a bonus. Recognizing it as duty, as Christians must, makes life not just difficult but well nigh impossible.

When Jesus came in the flesh, some people who heard Him preach and teach thought that He had come to replace the law, or to destroy it. Many people who consider themselves Christians today have the same misunderstanding. Especially in liberal theology, it is supposed that Jesus rescinded the law of the Old Testament and replaced it with a new operative principle: the law of love. The do's and don'ts of the Mosaic code were set aside, and a kind of fuzzy, humanistic, sentimental principle of "love" was instituted, which did away with particular commands and prohibitions. This wishful theology holds that Jesus, by repealing the Mosaic law with all of its sticky regulations and by instituting a more generalized law of love, made the matter of obedience to God a whole lot easier than it had been before His appearance. It is as though God saw fifteen hundred years of evidence that man could not keep the law, and so He simply had to make it easier, more manageable.

As in all heresy, there is a fragment of truth in this approach. Jesus did force His listeners to see beyond the particulars in the Mosaic law. He insisted that these particular rules and regulations were functions of greater principles, already identified in the Old Testament. He showed that the most important commandments were to "love the Lord your God with all your heart and with all your soul and with all your mind and with all your strength," and to "love your neighbor as yourself."[1] Love certainly was at the very heart of Jesus' message, no doubt about that. But what many fail to recognize is that (1) the various commands of the Mosaic law were expressions of that love for God and neighbor; (2) Jesus did not set the moral Law aside, but fulfilled it; and (3) by clarifying the greater principles upon which the Mosaic law had been built, Jesus removed the vain hopes of the Pharisees and others that they could in any way really keep, or be obedient to, the law.

For example, when Jesus talked about murder and adultery in the Sermon on the Mount, He did not lessen the demands of the moral Law. Rather, He proved that the moral Law was impossible for natural man to keep. He showed that it is not just the man who guns down another man who is guilty of murder: when you are angry with your brother you are subject to the same judgment. And He taught that merely looking at another woman lustfully is a violation of the Seventh Commandment.[2] The "law of love," though it boiled things down, showed that man's obligation to the law was considerably more than complying with lists of rules. Rather than announcing a new easy-believism, Jesus demonstrated that the demands of the law were further out of reach than most had supposed.

When we look at our ethical responsibility to the unborn child, we face this apparent impossibility of compliance. But our inadequacy is not limited to this issue. In reality, every obligation which we have before God, as His children, is greater than we can fulfill. We are commanded to go into all the world and preach the gospel too, but no one is capable of complete or perfect fulfillment of that charge. Scripture also tells us that pure religion, the kind that God accepts, is to look after orphans and widows in their distress and to keep oneself from being polluted by the world.[3] Can any man or woman legitimately claim that he has done enough for all the widows and orphans of the world? Who can say that he is altogether unpolluted by the world? When I have exhausted myself in my attempts to fulfill such ethical duties as set forth in Scripture, is there not still unfinished obligation? Likewise, no matter what measures I might take to protect or rescue my neighbor—the unborn child—there will still be more to do. There will still be obligation remaining unmet.

To demonstrate this, we need only look at those who have taken the most extreme measures in this regard in the present day. Consider Joan Andrews. She recognizes that what she has done, in and of itself, has had (sadly) too little an effect on the lives of the unborn, at least from a numerical standpoint. It is impossible for Joan Andrews to be everywhere, to clog up the passageway at every abortion clinic, or even for that matter to keep abortions from taking place at one clinic for very long. The job is just too immense. How can I be a real neighbor to the unborn, as Scripture requires? Even assuming that I am willing to "pay the cost" in terms of personal sacrifices, will my efforts really be effective?

If Biblical answers to that question are to be given, it is important first to recognize clearly where it is that the Christian obtains the power to obey God in any area of his life. The question is: how is a man to please God? Fulfilling the ethical demands of Scripture is really equivalent to holiness. And a man is no more capable of fulfilling that demand which is placed upon him than he is of saving himself. As he was utterly unable to bring himself to faith apart from God's grace, so he is entirely incapable of fulfilling the Biblical ethical mandate on his own. The late John Murray wrote:

One feature of the witness of Scripture that bears directly upon the biblical ethic is its teaching on the depravity of human nature. "There is none righteous, no, not one. . . . There is none that doeth good, no, not even one" (Romans 3:10, 12). According to the Bible human depravity is such that the fulfilment of the demands of the biblical ethic is an impossibility. The mind of the flesh, the mind of the natural man, "is not subject to the law of God, neither indeed can it be" (Romans 8:7). It is this impossibility that makes necessary the provisions of redemptive grace. In relation to the ethic of Scripture the question then becomes: How are the provisions of redemptive grace brought to bear upon the fulfilment of ethical demand?

The answer is that we men must be brought within the orbit of the forces of redemption. . . .[4]

What Murray is saying is basically what the Apostle Paul said in his letter to the Galatian Christians. The redemptive work of God's grace in justification (that point in time when a man is reconciled to God in Christ) is the same redemptive work of God's free grace that sanctifies (the process of the renewal of a justified man, in which he is made more and more to conform to the image of Christ). Both justification and sanctification are entirely works of God's free grace. We obtain both through faith alone. The two are, in substance, the same work of "salvation."

Many of us, as we have come to understand these truths, have often applied them in too restricted a way. We have applied them internally, to the individual Christian only. Certainly this is the primary and most obvious application. Justification and holy living are personal matters. But this process of holiness—of godly, obedient living—will of necessity have effects outside the Christian's individual life. The brand of sanctification to which God calls the Christian is both internal and external. As long as the Christian is in the world, obedience to Christ means much more than a personal pietism, important and foundational as that may be. The Good Samaritan had more than himself to be concerned about. There was that man by the side of the road. The Christian's piety, his holiness, is defined in terms of others as well as himself. God's redemptive power is at work outside, as well as inside, the Christian.

Sanctification—the gracious work of God to make us holy—is a process. It has both internal and external ramifications. As an internal work, Scripture often describes it as affecting the "heart" of the believer. Here it is that man's will is changed. The Holy Spirit brings about changed dispositions: faith, hope, and love. A man's motivations are changed; his affections are made over.[5] But the other aspect of sanctification is equally important: the changed life. The changed heart means I desire to love God and my neighbor; the changed life means that I love God and my neighbor in fact, in real actions, in historical events. Herman Ridderbos puts it this way:

Therefore, the heart is on the one hand the point of impact of the Holy
Spirit, and it is there that the great decisions fall; but it is also clear
that renewal by the Spirit does not confine itself to the heart of the inward man, but intends from thence to determine his entire humanity
as well.[6]

My ethical responsibility to my neighbor is part of the process of
holy living, because it is part of obedience to Christ. It is part of the
renewal of the whole man. Thus the process of fulfilling Christian
ethical responsibility in the world, because it is part of sanctification, is a product of God's grace, and is obtained through faith alone.

When Murray says that we must be brought within the "orbit of
the forces of redemption," he is talking about a great deal more than
the power of God in justifying the sinner when he was initially
brought to faith in Christ. That is, of course, the initial step and the
first evidence of God's irresistible grace in his life; unless he is so
justified, a man cannot please God because he does not have the
supernatural power of the Holy Spirit in his life. But the point is that
redemptive grace does not end at conversion. Everything that a man
does, from the time of his conversion on, if it is to be pleasing to God
and truly helpful to his neighbor, will be exclusively a product of
God's redemptive grace. It is not just our*selves* that get redeemed;
it is also our work. Our righteousness (ethical fulfillment) will come
about as a result of God's grace. David understood this:

> Commit your way to the Lord;
>   trust in him and he will do this:
> He will make your righteousness shine like the dawn,
>   the justice of your cause like the noonday sun.[7]

In summary, God's grace is to be applied not only in our justification, nor only in the transformation of our inward affections, but
also in the actualization of His righteousness in ourselves and in the
world around us.

It is essential that we grasp this truth because if we do not, our
attempts to please God in service to others, our efforts to establish
justice and mercy in the world will come to nothing. Particularizing
this truth to the matter at hand, if Christians are not appropriating the
power of God's redemptive grace as the backbone of their undertak-

ings to win justice for the unborn, their efforts, no matter how humanitarian and otherwise well-motivated, will fail.

This is particularly important to understand as we participate in the actual day-to-day work in the pro-life movement, in every sphere of the effort. Whether it is manning a telephone hotline, working as an adoption agency volunteer, distributing literature, writing legislation, representing activists in court, sitting in at the abortion clinic, or whatever the duty that is undertaken, the work is typically sacrificial in nature. There is usually no pay, few accolades, and generous criticism. It is easy to fall back into a theological economy of works. We easily forget the inadequacy of our own abilities while immersing ourselves in our own busyness, failing to avail ourselves of the redemptive power of God in bringing success to our efforts. When we begin to believe that somehow it is through our works that this battle is to be fought and won, we have already lost.

If we are to triumph in this battle for justice, it will be a triumph of faith. It is at its core a spiritual battle, and it must be fought with spiritual weapons. But here there is great potential for error. By calling the battle "spiritual," we can quickly retreat from action. We can adopt a bare pietism, claiming that all God wants of us is to preach and pray. We fail to understand that a battle which is fought with spiritual weapons, a battle of faith, is one which almost always involves action. Biblical faith is expressed in action, not just in words.

Hebrews 11 is the famous text on the subject of faith. Here the inspired writer gives historical reports of individuals, spanning history from Adam's son Abel on down through the exhilic prophets, who were men and women of faith. How are they characterized? It is significant that hardly a word of these champions of faith is quoted. These are men and women who are remembered primarily for what they did. Abel offered a better sacrifice than Cain; Noah built an ark on dry ground; Abraham moved his family from his homeland and lived in tents; Rahab hid the spies. When the writer recognizes that the details regarding each character may become too lengthy, he summarizes:

And what more shall I say? I do not have time to tell about Gideon, Barak, Samson, Jephthah, David, Samuel and the prophets, who through faith conquered kingdoms, administered justice, and gained what was promised; who shut the mouths of lions, quenched the fury of the flames, and escaped the edge of the sword; whose weakness was turned to strength; and who became powerful in battle and routed foreign armies. Women received back their dead, raised to life again. . . .[8]

When we remember the Old Testament patriarchs, the judges, the prophets, and the other heroic men and women, we tend to dwell on their spectacular, often miraculous works, many of which are listed in this passage. The mouths of the lions were miraculously shut for Daniel; the fury of the flames was quenched for his friends Shadrach, Meshach, and Abednego. These were the great, dazzling events of the Old Testament that are rightfully prominent in our memories, partly because they are the stories that filled our Bible story books and Sunday school classes as children.

But there is an unexpected phrase in that series of miracles wrought by faith. Right alongside the lions' den and the fiery furnace is the administration of justice. We tend to think of the administration of justice as the norm, even in our sinful world. We do not usually think of justice as a miracle. As we read the news day by day, we often see the deprivation of human rights (abortion, the Soviets in Afghanistan, apartheid—whatever the news story) as the deviation from a worldly norm. We assume that most men in the world are basically interested in and capable of bringing justice to their countries and people.

It is true that God has distributed a basic sense of justice to all men. Men have a measure of human love for one another; parents who are not Christians love their children. These are aspects of God's common grace. The Apostle Paul states in Romans 2 that the Gentiles, apart from God's special revelation, nevertheless are a "law for themselves, even though they do not have the [moral] law," and that they thus display that they have the law written on their hearts.[9] But this imprinting of the law on the heart of natural man is very soon suppressed, perverted, obscured, and debilitated by sin, as explained in Romans 1. True justice is something which those who are estranged from Jehovah God cannot produce on their own, and apart from God's grace do not really want to produce. Bringing real justice to this broken world—the establishment of Biblical human rights—requires supernatural power, the same power that gave women back their dead, raised to life again. The power to bring justice and mercy to bear in society today is the same power by which Elijah gave the widow at Zarephath back her only son after he had died—it is resurrection power.[10] It is a power that is appropriated to us and to our twentieth-century life by faith.

The administration of justice requires God's supernatural power, but this passage in Hebrews implies something further. We need to remember that some of those who wrought these things were tortured, some faced jeers and flogging, some were chained and put into prison. Some were stoned, some sawed in two, some put to death by the sword. An enterprise of faith is a battle with the enemy. It is an all-out battle, not just fine-tuning a situation that has gotten a little out of adjustment.

Practically speaking, how can God's redemptive power be brought to bear in our battle for the unborn? First let us say how it will not be brought to bear. It will not be brought to bear through unbelief, through what J. I. Packer calls the "nervous, dithery, take-no-risks mood that mars so much of our discipleship." God's grace, God's help, will come through faith. That is the only way: faith demonstrated by obedient action. As we venture forth into the battle for the unborn, there are three components of this faith that are vital for our survival and for our success:

First, we must recognize that God is sovereign in the affairs of men. This truth is the cornerstone of Christian action. And the Christian holds that all God's power has been given to Jesus Christ. We must remember that

> by him all things were created: things in heaven and on earth, visible and invisible, whether thrones or powers or rulers or authorities; all things were created by him and for him. He is before all things, and in him all things hold together.[11]

The odds may seem to be heavily stacked against us, and all of us (not just the trespassers!) may be made to feel that we are treading on someone else's territory much of the time. We are not; it is all God's turf. And while it has not been given to us to impose obedience to God upon all men and human institutions, we can take confidence that He holds the heart of the king in His hand. As I counsel on the sidewalk outside the abortion clinic, I can confidently remember that my Lord created everything I see; that He even made—in His image—the abortionists I see going into the building; that He made the escorts hired by the clinic to provide safe passage to the mothers who are seeking abortions. As I go into the courtroom to defend my clients who attempted to rescue the unborn child, I remember that God is not tagging along reluctantly, wondering what this secular business is all about, but that He is the very One who has established the authority of the court system, and that the judge has no power at all over me or my clients if it is not given to him from above.[12] I remember that this is my Father's world—not "I hope to make it so," but "I rest me in the thought." Faith always involves this recognition of God's sovereignty. It produces not an attitude of arrogance, but one of peace, confidence, joy, humility, and awe. And it is the fact of God's sovereignty that gives substance and encouragement to our prayerful obedience to His will.

Second, we must base our work on prayer. Prayer is premised on God's sovereignty. It is because He is absolutely in control of every aspect of the created order that we can pray confidently. God's control is absolute; His power is infinite. Prayer is His appointed means of our accessing His power: prayer is a means of grace. By His grace, we are invited—even commanded—to pray for His will to be done on earth, even as it is in Heaven. From Genesis to Revelation we see that God's work was accomplished, that God's will was effected in the affairs of the world—through prayer. Why would we expect any lasting success in the pro-life effort apart from prayer?

What should we pray for? Our prayers need to be specific. Specific prayers bring specific answers. Our prayers also need to be bold; while it is important that we always pray within the context of "Thy will be done," we can and should risk making a mistake once in a while in a request. God can handle that. Risk praying along these lines:

(1) Pray daily for the unborn children of your community. Ask God to intervene on their behalf, to protect them from death.

(2) Get the names and addresses of the abortion clinics in your area (you can usually get this information from the Yellow Pages). Pray daily that God would close them down. Argue to God that children are being slaughtered there, that innocent life is being taken,

that you are like Lot who, living among lawless men day after day, was tormented in his righteous soul by the lawless deeds he saw and heard.[13] Tell God that you cannot stand this atrocity, and that you want Him to intervene.

(3) Get the names of the abortionist doctors. This information is harder to obtain, but you could attempt it by calling the abortion clinic itself and asking for the names of the doctors. If you cannot get it that way, get in touch with one of your local pro-life organizations, and get a list of the names of the abortionists. Pray that God would turn them away from bloodshed, and pray that He would bring them to the light.

(4) From your local pro-life organization, obtain a list of the hospitals in your area that perform abortions. Pray specifically, naming the particular hospital, that God would bring an end to that practice there.

(5) Pray for the Supreme Court.[14] Pray specifically that *Roe v. Wade* might be reversed. Pray regarding those justices on the Supreme Court who have gone on record time and time again as supporting abortion. Ask God to mercifully remove them from such a position of authority in our country. Pray this for William J. Brennan, Jr., Thurgood Marshall, Harry A. Blackmun, and John Paul Stevens. Pray that they will either be changed in their position or replaced by men or women who will honor the image of God, who will protect the lives of the unborn. Express to God your sense of urgency in the matter. Pray for the other justices also, that they will be given wisdom above their own, and that they will consistently vote against permitting abortion.

(6) Pray for the President, as he is the one who makes appointments to the Supreme Court, and for the Senate, which approves or disapproves his choices. Pray that God will give these individuals wisdom above their own in their selections. Pray for Congress and for your state legislature, that there will be a quickening of interest and concern about the abortion issue; that laws will be passed limiting, controlling, and ultimately forbidding abortion again.

(7) Pray especially for yourself. Pray that God would give you specific opportunity to increase your involvement in the pro-life effort, making use of your particular position in life and your gifts. Tell Him that you desire to be involved in the working out of the answers to your prayers in 1-4. Pray that you might have more

concern for the helpless unborn, for wisdom in determining how best to intervene, for specific opportunities to do so, for courage.

(8) Pray for those who are in prison.[15] Get acquainted with Christians in your locality who have interposed themselves on behalf of the unborn at abortion clinics, and pray with and for them. Pray for the success of their efforts, and if you are one who joins in those efforts, cover all of your planned activities in prayer. And after you have acted, continue to pray that God will "establish the work of our hands."[16] That is, ask that God will honor your attempts to be obedient, that He will ratify them and bring results.

Obviously, this list could go on and on. The point is that all of the specific goals of the effort to protect the child at the clinic, to reinstate protection for the unborn child, must be first and foremost matters of prayer. No activity should be undertaken without prayer. And this takes time. It is hard work. It is not popular. But it is very effective, and it is dangerous because it usually leads the Christian to increased levels of service.

Third, we must act in humble but fearless obedience to God. Prayer and obedient action go hand in hand. As we pray, we move toward increased integrity before God in our actions. As we take action, we discover more and more need for prayer. This is the life of faith: prayerful obedience to what God has commanded.

As we consider the particular actions to which we are called, we must view our responsibility through the eyes of the unborn child. To the extent we can do so, we must put ourselves in his position. What kind of help would I want if I faced what he is facing? What kind of help would be appropriate or adequate?

The precise particulars of action which the individual must take are in large part dependent upon his gifts, his sphere of activity. But that is not to say that the action which each must take in this matter is entirely subjective. We have seen the ethical demand set forth in Scripture. The requirement is obedience for every one of us. The requirement is integrity for every one of us. The requirement is that we treat the unborn child with integrity, as we would want to be treated ourselves. To accomplish that measure of obedience, we must prayerfully depend on God's grace in us and in His world around us. He will bring it to pass; the battle is the Lord's.

OBJECTIONS CONSIDERED

*M*any Christians have raised various objections to their brothers and sisters who have disobeyed the civil law at the doors of abortion clinics. Many objections have been discussed along the way in the foregoing chapters, but it may be helpful to catalog some of the most frequent of these objections (at least those of which this author is aware) and to respond to each.

Almost all of these objections have been formulated as answers to questions raised by members of local American evangelical congregations. Some of these Christians (laymen and clergymen alike) have debated whether or not they should venture into the fray and become some of those who are willing to go to jail to protect the lives of the unborn. They have looked to church leadership for answers before they did so. Thus, some of these objections have had real-life significance for people who have considered their personal responsibilities in the battle for the unborn. It is crucial to give reasoned and Biblical responses to such objections.

I am convinced that those who have raised these criticisms are for the most part honestly seeking Scriptural answers to the issues discussed in this book. In this era of viewing truth "through a glass darkly," we will have strong differences of opinion, even on important issues.

And yet, while we humbly confess to a less than perfect understanding of Scripture, where Scripture does speak clearly we have no right to pretend that the clear truth spoken in Scripture is still somehow competing against our contradictory opinions. If we are satisfied that Scripture speaks clearly on these matters, we must align our hearts, minds, and actions with that truth, and not claim that simply because others within the Christian community disagree, objective truth on the matter is unattainable. Each criticism must be weighed carefully and prudently, in the light of all of Scripture, with the prayerful expectation that the Holy Spirit will give us a clear sense of direction. We must "take captive every thought to make it obedient to Christ."[1]

The objections here listed are stated, as closely as possible, in the words of those who have framed them. Particular effort has been made to avoid the temptation to set these concerns up as "straw men" for easy and neat responses.

Objection 1: The law under *Roe v. Wade* does not require the Christian to sin by having an abortion. The Christian should disobey the civil law only when the state requires that he personally disobey God.

Response: The justification for illegal intervention at the door of the abortion clinic does not arise directly out of the fact that abortion is sin. Rather, the justification arises out of the positive obligation which the Christian has to the unborn child. To fail to intervene on behalf of the child is a failure of Christian duty. The Christian cannot yield to the state where the state forbids his fulfillment of Christian duty. In this sense, the Christian is indeed justified in "resisting" the state—but it is not a generalized resistance to governmental authority. It is carefully bracketed by the extent and limits of Christian duty as defined in Scripture.

This objection fails to recognize that sin is characterized both by commission and omission. Obtaining an abortion would be a sin of commission; failing to help another person in the fulfillment of Christian duty is a sin of omission.

Objection 2: Women who elect abortion, and the doctors who perform the procedure, are free moral agents, and are responsible for their acts. Though abortion is sin (and a very grievous one, because it is the taking of another human being's life), it is no different in kind from un-Biblical divorce, profanity, or gossip. Christians are not called upon to act as "vigilantes," contrary to the civil law, in attempting to stamp out the sin of others.

Response: This objection mentions only two of the participants in an abortion: the mother and the abortionist doctor. There is no question but that these two participants are fully responsible for their acts, or that their sin, however heinous, is something for which they must answer. However, the objection fails to mention the third "participant" in an abortion: the child. It is true that the Christian is not called upon (as we have said earlier) to make citizens' arrests for the Kingdom of Heaven; but he is required to show the love of Christ to others—including unborn children—to preserve and protect their lives. Not only is this a demand that God places upon us, but it is something which, by the indwelling of the Holy Spirit, the child of God will desire to do.

Abortion is by its nature somewhat unique as a moral wrong because there is no space between the sin and the damage caused by the sin. The unborn child intrinsically, immediately, and irretrievably becomes the victim of the evil. Thus protection of the victim (which is part of Christian duty) will always appear to be a policing of someone's sin (which is not mandated as part of Christian duty). For example, there is more distance between the sins of divorce, profanity, pornography, or gossip and their victims, more opportunity for remedial help and intervention, more retrievability. We could say (theoretically) that we block the entrance to an abortion clinic not to stop the sin of abortion, but to protect the victim of abortion. I say "theoretically" because it is obvious that stopping the sin of abortion is necessary to the protection of the victim.

Objection 3: If we were under theocratic rule, such as Israel was in Old Testament times, we could justify the imposition of God's Law on others. But we cannot force others to live by God's Law in a secular or pagan society such as we have in the United States today.

Response: It is agreed that whatever justification there is for civil disobedience in resistance to abortion, it cannot be based upon some notion of theocratic rule. We do not live in a theocracy. As noted in our answer to Objection 2, the rationale is not to police the mother's or the abortionist's sin; it is not to impose God's Law on these participants, but to recognize and obey God's Law on us, as citizens of the Kingdom of Heaven. It is our duty, not the world's duty, that is at issue.

Most of the illustrations of civil disobedience in Scripture, where men obeyed God rather than men, were in nontheocratic, pagan systems of government. Daniel, Shadrach, Meshach, and Abednego were under the law of Babylon; the Hebrew midwives were under the law of Egypt; Rahab was under the law of the king of Jericho; Peter and the apostles were under the law of Rome. As discussed in Chapter Four, whenever any government commands the Christian to violate God's commands, or forbids him from Christian duty, he must obey God rather than men. Thus, our resistance to abortion and our responsibility to actively protect the lives of the unborn are not so much a function of the laws or philosophical moorings of the nation or state in which we live. Our responsibility to the unborn should be the same in the United States, France, India, the U.S.S.R., or China.

Objection 4: Pro-life activists claim a positive duty to rescue the unborn baby, based on Proverbs 24:11, 12:

> Rescue those being led away to death;
>   hold back those staggering toward slaughter.
> If you say, "But we knew nothing about this,"
>   does not he who weighs the heart perceive it?
> Does not he who guards your life know it?
> Will he not repay each person
>   according to what he has done?

But in so doing (the objection continues) pro-life activists take the passage out of context and misapply it. First, the verses have spiritual (not physical or biological) application. Second, the verses do not command or permit the violation of the civil law. And third, to so apply the passage would mean that the Christian should intervene all over the world, in other kinds of situations, to save lives.

Response: There is no compelling reason to assume that the Proverbs passage should not be taken literally. Because of the literary style of Proverbs (lists of short statements of moral and ethical truth compiled in sometimes unrelated sequence) it is difficult to prove much from the context. But the words are straightforward, and although they may have a "spiritual" dimension ("slaughter" meaning, say, eternal damnation), the primary application still would be physical death, physical slaughter, physical life.

But it also needs to be emphasized that this passage, which is widely used in the pro-life movement, is not the only Scriptural authority which posits an affirmative duty on the child of God to preserve and protect the life of others. Christians who raise this objection hopefully would not seriously hold that if the Proverbs passage somehow could be shown to be inapplicable to children being killed by abortion, we would be off the hook on that part of Christian duty. The major and minor prophets' writings and proclamations are full of charges against Judah and Israel for their failures to defend the innocent, to protect innocent blood. It was for these sins, in large part, that the two nations of Israel were judged and sent into captivity. Isaiah described the ethical duty of the follower of Jehovah in terms of a fast:

> Is not this the kind of fasting I have chosen:
>   to loose the chains of injustice
>   and untie the cords of the yoke,
>   to set the oppressed free
>   and break every yoke?
> Is it not to share your food with the hungry
>   and to provide the poor wanderer with shelter—
>   when you see the naked, to clothe him,
>   and not to turn away from your own flesh and blood?[2]

As argued in Chapters Four and Five, this principle of concerned action on behalf of those who cannot help themselves is restated and confirmed in the preaching of Jesus, particularly in the parable of the Good Samaritan, and this law of love, growing out of love for God, constitutes the summary of the law and the prophets.

As to the "objection" that a literal interpretation of this passage would result in placement of a burden on Christians to protect lives in situations other than abortion, there will be no disagreement. Duty cannot logically be disproved simply because the burden seems too heavy. No one has claimed that Proverbs 24:11, 12 should be limited to abortion in its application. Abortion, unlike suffering in other parts of the world, is close at hand. Abortion, unlike capital punishment, involves unquestionably innocent and helpless human lives. Abortion, unlike street crime, is carried out at scheduled times and at particular addresses. If innocent human lives are being taken other than by abortion, at a certain place and time in your commu-

nity, it is obvious that as a Christian you would have an equal duty
to do what you could to protect those lives.

The Proverbs passage does not speak to the issue of civil
disobedience, and thus cannot be used in isolation as a prooftext for
or against it.

Objection 5: If we disobey the law by sitting in front of the
doors of an abortion clinic, where will we stop? If the justification
for such an act is that the baby's life is worthy of protection, just as
a born child's life would be worthy of protection, why should we not
also justify armed intervention, or kidnapping and detention of the
abortionist, or the bombing of abortion clinics and similar activities?

Response: At the outset, it should be observed that whatever
hypothetical extensions may be placed upon our arguments, in point
of fact the "rescue" activists have by and large preached and practiced nonviolence. Violence at the abortion clinic, in resistance to
abortion, is not the phenomenon confronting us. We are confronted,
for the most part, with nonviolent attempts to intervene on behalf of
the unborn child. It is not entirely fair to oppose a practice simply
because it may lead to an extreme measure that is disavowed by
current activists.

The Operation Rescue organization requires that participants
in a rescue sign the following pledge:[3]

PLEDGE FOR ON-SITE PARTICIPATION
I understand the critical importance of Operation Rescue being unified, peaceful, and free of any actions or words that would appear violent or hateful to those watching the event on TV or reading about it
in a newspaper.

I realize that some pro-abortion elements of the media desire to
discredit Rescues (and then the whole pro-life movement) and focus
on a side issue, in order to avoid the central issue at hand—murdered
children.

Hence, I understand that for the children's sake, each Rescue must
be orderly and above reproach.

Therefore . . .

I will cooperate with the spirit and goals of Operation Rescue, as
explained by the leadership.

I commit to be peaceful and nonviolent in both word and deed.

Should I be arrested, I will not struggle with police in any way (whether deed or tongue), but remain polite and passively limp, remembering that mercy triumphs over judgment.

I will follow the instructions of the Operation Rescue crowd control marshals.

I understand that certain individuals will be appointed to speak to the media, the police, and the women seeking abortion. I will not take it upon myself to yell out to anyone, but will continue singing and praying with the main group, as directed.

I sign this pledge, having seriously considered what I do, and with the determination and will to persevere by the grace of God.

_____
Signature

_____
Date

Pro-choice advocates love to criticize pro-life activists for supposedly employing "terrorist" tactics. In that way, attention is shifted from the brutal, daily violence in the abortion industry, which Paul Fowler has depicted:

> The methods of abortion are physically violent. Whether it be a sharp, double-edged curette (or knife) by which the child is unceremoniously dissected, or the suction of the inserted tube which tears apart the tiny child, or the burning effect of the injected saline solution on the tender skin of the child while simultaneously poisoning the baby internally—there is no term more appropriate for such cruel methods than violence.[4]

This is mentioned not to justify the use of violent means to resist abortion, but to maintain perspective. In this objection, the pro-life activist is being asked to answer for violence which he has disavowed. To use potential future violence as an argument against a present peaceful effort to halt actual present violence is preposterous.

Pro-life activists who undertake rescue missions have elected the nonviolent approach for many reasons, among them:

(1) It is difficult to imagine any form of violence that does not

involve substantial risk to the lives of individuals. Obviously, the bombing of abortion clinics endangers any lives in the proximity of the blast, including those having nothing to do with the abortion clinic. Setting fire to an abortion clinic runs the same risk, and in most states if a life of a firefighter, for example, were taken in the efforts to extinguish the blaze, the arsonist could be charged with murder under the felony-murder law. Such risk of life is contrary to the very foundation of the pro-life movement.

(2) Intentional violence against individuals, by its nature, is punitive or penal in nature. Nonviolent interposition of my body between the unborn baby and the abortionist is not punitive or penal. It has been given to government to act as "an agent of wrath to bring punishment on the wrongdoer,"[5] and an individual has no independent authority to mete out punishment to others.

(3) The objective in the rescue at the abortion clinic is to save children. If enough people are involved, rescues can be carried out successfully without the employment of violent means.

Objection 6: We must recognize that our Sovereign God has His purposes. If it is His will to bring judgment upon the ungodly by letting them bring on their own destruction through abortion (no one is imposing it upon Christians), should we interfere with His judgment? After all, unborn babies (as well as born children) were destroyed in Noah's flood, in Sodom and Gomorrah, and in Joshua's conquest of Canaan. We must honestly, realistically, and humbly face this question: are we justified in making indiscriminate attempts to save unborn babies? The children whose lives we would save at the abortion clinic are probably mostly children of unbelievers. There is no Biblical reference to any rescue efforts being made by the Israelites, or even the prophets of Israel, in the Old Testament when the pagan families around them were offering their children to Molech. While we may have an obligation to perform "rescues" within the covenant community, there is no Biblical warrant for doing it outside the family of believers.

Response: This objection is a perversion of Covenant Theology, its necessary implication being that the blessing of (or right to) physical life is something which may be limited to offspring of Christians; that our concerns for justice do not extend beyond the community of believers into the world; that the Golden Rule ("do unto others as you would have them do unto you") and the second great commandment to love your neighbor as yourself have reference only to other believers and their children.

The logical consequence of this objection is that the Sixth Commandment, "Thou shalt not kill," does not protect the lives of unbelievers, but only those of believers. Presumably if Scripture allows us to turn away from the plight of the children of unbelievers, it would allow us to actively take their lives as well.

This objection also assumes facts not in evidence. There is no Biblical data informing us of the Israelites' failure to intervene on behalf of Canaanite babies being sacrificed in the fires of Molech; there is no record of God's affirmation of their failure to intervene; there is no mention of the proximity of the infant human sacrifices to the homes of the Israelites. We do not know if there were twenty-three or twenty-three million babies killed in this way. A theology of nonintervention should not be constructed on such sparse evidence. By contrast, as we have argued, there is an abundance of Scriptural evidence concerning the duty of Christians to preserve and protect the lives of others—"others" being all those made in the image of God.

This objection would question whether Christians such as Corrie ten Boom and her family were justified in housing Jewish babies in their home during the Nazi Holocaust. This too was an "indiscriminate" rescue effort. The Good Samaritan would also come in for some criticism: he did not ask the victim by the side of the road if he was a believer before he lent a hand.

Objection 7: Christians should not use civil disobedience to restore God's order to society, because they will then become dependent upon such measures and will always look to activism as the method of change.

Response: If the battle for the unborn is indeed won, Christians on that happy day will realize as they take their armor off that it was not won merely because of the success of activism. It will be because of God's gracious intervention. But more importantly, the objective of the civilly disobedient act of the Christian is not primarily "to restore God's order to society" or to force a change in the law. There is usually no hidden agenda in the mind of the rescuer: his act is an act of conscience, motivated by his concern for the life of the child. It arises out of his obedience to Christ and is propelled by his love for Christ.

Objection 8: The law being broken by the pro-life activist (the law forbidding trespass) has nothing whatsoever to do with abortion. Those arrested are not being arrested because they are protesting abortion. If certain anti-God protesters blocked the entrance to our churches, so we could not worship, we would use the same ordinance to have them arrested.

Response: This objection is based upon the assumption that civil disobedience is always designed and employed to change a particularly unjust law by disobeying that law, forcing prosecution of that law, gaining publicity, and raising the level of public con-science so that pressure is brought to bear to get the unjust law changed (e.g., a black being prosecuted and jailed for sitting in one of the front seats of a city bus in the 1950s). We have not considered whether such a model of civil disobedience is permissible for the Christian or not. For that traditional model espoused, among others, by the late Martin Luther King, Jr.,[6] violation of the law was the essential act in obtaining a change in the law. Not so in Operation Rescue. For the one who intervenes for the child at the abortion clinic, violation of the law is incidental to the essential act: rescuing the child. If the children could be rescued legally (as they often are), there would happily be no illegal act. This is not to say that public-ity, public conscience, confrontation with the powers that be, and other aspects of traditional civil disobedience are not present in the rescue efforts. They are unquestionably there. The point is that they are not foremost, and they are not essential to the purpose of the action taken.

This objection is the argument given often by trial judges when rescuers are being tried for trespass. In these cases the court will many times refuse to permit evidence regarding abortion or evidence showing the particular purpose for which the defendant was at the scene, on the grounds that such evidence is immaterial to the ele-ments of a trespass charge. Normally the only facts to be determined in a trespass case are whether the defendant was on another's prop-erty and whether or not the defendant left the property when the owner or his agent told him to leave. But the argument that the rescuers try to raise is that their trespass was justified, and that they therefore should be found "not guilty," because they were on the property of another only to save a life in immediate danger. This is the defense of "justification" or "necessity," normally recognized as a defense in American law, but currently judged by courts as unavailable to trespassers at abortion clinics because of the constitutional right to abortion under *Roe v. Wade* (see discussion in Chapter Eight).

It also needs to be said that the seemingly unrelated law of trespass, through its enforcement and application at the door of the abortion clinic, becomes very substantially related to the morality of abortion itself. As applied by enforcement in a particular circumstance, a law can take on moral dimensions not evident on its face.

In April 1953, when I was nine years old, my six-year-old sister Mary had what we believed was the flu. She was sick with nausea and had a very high fever. We lived in rural Iowa, and our family doctor, a member of the church my father pastored, lived and practiced in Cedar Rapids, about twenty-five miles from our home. After Mary had endured about a week of sickness, it came to a crisis when she developed a "doubling up" kind of pain in her abdomen. Dad called Dr. Sloan; even though he was chief of surgeons at the hospital where he was on staff, he rushed out to our home. His diagnosis was instant: ruptured appendix. It was a life-and-death situation for Mary. I remember vividly how this good doctor swept this little drawn, white-faced girl up into his arms, ran down the steps with her, and rushed out to his car. He quickly laid her on the backseat and sped off.

The rest of the story was told to us later. Dr. Sloan knew that every second counted if Mary's life were to be saved. He drove between 80 and 110 miles per hour all the way from our home to the city, on a two-lane road. He continued at these high speeds when he reached the outskirts of Cedar Rapids, where the speed limit was 30 miles per hour. He heard sirens and saw red lights flashing and an officer pulled him over. Dr. Sloan barely stopped, rolled down his window, pointed to his precious cargo in the backseat, and shouted out an explanation of his mission. The policeman ran back to the squad car and now, instead of pursuing a speeder, provided an escort to the hospital so that the life of a little girl could be saved. Her life was saved—narrowly. After many complications, a month later Mary returned from the hospital to a very thankful family.

What if the officer had looked in the backseat of the car and then grimly shaken his head, all the while apologizing for the fact that he didn't write the laws, but just enforced them, and that speeding was an offense that he was assigned to handle? What if he had arrested Dr. Sloan, taken him to the station, fingerprinted and booked him, put him in a holdover tank until his friends could raise his bond, all while Mary perished in the backseat of the car? Would the enforcement of the speeding laws of Cedar Rapids in that instance have been morally neutral? And what if later, in court, Dr. Sloan defended himself on the speeding charge by attempting to bring in the fact that he had had a sick and dying girl in the backseat of his car, stating that his reason for speeding was that he needed to get her to the hospital for surgery—does anyone really think that evidence should be excluded by the court because it is unrelated to the speeding ordinance?

Is the effort made by Dr. Sloan substantially different from the illegal rescue missions at abortion clinics? If we sense a difference, it is probably because we can see Mary in the backseat of the doctor's car. If she were to be removed from our view, either because she really was not there, or because we somehow chose to ignore her while we argued, say, about a doctor's constitutional right to speed, then the law of speeding would become the only real issue in Dr. Sloan's trial.

The law against speeding, and the law against trespass, enforced in certain circumstances, become great moral and legal issues. It is the little girl in a predicament in the backseat of the car that makes all the difference.

APPENDIX A

THE DUTY OF DISOBEDIENCE TO WICKED LAWS*
by Charles Beecher (1851)

There is to be a day of judgment—a day when God will reveal His righteous judgment concerning all deeds done in the body. In that review no part of human conduct will be exempt from scrutiny. The public as well as the private acts of every man will undergo impartial examination. Nor will the acts of individuals, only, be considered. The acts of organic bodies of men constitute a very large part of all history, and must be judged. The acts of nations, governments, and all authorities will be diligently examined; and especially the laws which were by different nations passed, accepted, obeyed. . . .

My object tonight will be to take such a view of the late Fugitive Slave Law, passed by the Congress of these United States, and approved by the President. I wish to inquire how that law will look when examined before the bar of God. I wish to ask how the men that made it, the men that execute, the citizens that obey, and the nation that tolerates that law, will look when they stand before the judgment seat. And,

I observe that laws are to be judged of by certain principles of natural right, and by those same principles as more clearly evolved in the gospel—that gospel, I mean, which was preached before Moses, as well as after. (Gal. 3:8).

These principles of right are eternal, not made. They are the foundation of law, not its product. . . . God's legislation is declaratory of what is absolutely right. Man's legislation is declaratory of

*Charles Beecher, *The Duty of Disobedience to Wicked Laws* (Newark, NJ, 1851). Charles Beecher was brother to Harriet Beecher Stowe, author of *Uncle Tom's Cabin*. He became a Presybterian minister in Indiana in 1844, but moved to Newark, New Jersey, as a minister in the First Congregational Church in that city. In that same year he was expelled from the ministerial association of which he had become a member, for preaching the sermon from which excerpts are here reprinted.

what he conceives to be right. Hence human law is nothing but a declaration of the public idea of right; or, at least, it can rise no higher than the public idea. Of course, then, as the public idea of right is obscure and progressive, law must be progressive. Ancient laws are now seen to have been barbarous, not because they had not some elements of right, but because they had some elements of wrong admixed. Hence modern laws continually amend, supersede, or annul laws that are older. And just in proportion as the national intellect and conscience are developed, just in proportion as man returns toward the image and likeness of God, will this process of improved legislation be apparent.

Hence the mind of man is destined to be always testing its own legislation by those principles on which God tests it and will render verdict in the judgment. For, in the language of Sir William Blackstone, "The law of nature, being coeval with mankind and dictated by God Himself, is of course superior in obligation to any other. It is binding all over the globe, in all countries, at all times; no human laws are of any validity if contrary to this; and such of them as are valid derive all their force, and all their validity, mediately or immediately, from this original." . . .

This law then is wrong in the sight of God and man—it is an unexampled climax of sin. It is the monster iniquity of the present age, and it will stand forever on the page of history, as the vilest monument of infamy of the nineteenth century. Russia knows nothing like it. . . .

[But] there is yet one thing more guilty than the act of passing this law. There is yet one step wanting to render complete and awful in the sight of God our mighty guilt; and that step is obedience to the law. That is a sin even more exquisitely sinful than the making of the law itself, for two reasons: first, because it has the whole atrociousness of the law itself; and secondly, because it has the whole atrociousness of a stab at the freedom of conscience, and of private judgment. . . .

Why does any man imagine he ought to obey the law? What is the Jesuitical plea which is industriously inculcated by the high priests of Moloch and Mammon? It is because he wants to keep on the safe side, by obeying law. Because he is told that the proper way is to obey, until the law can be altered. Because he is told it is wrong to do right, unless the Government gives him leave—right to do wrong, whenever an aristocracy of politicians, and a hierarchy of office-holders, command. Because he pins his faith on the sleeve of Government, and makes Congress his pope, cardinals, and holy college of Jesuits, to act the part of infallible interpreter for him, of the Bible and of duty. This is the reason, and the only reason why he obeys. The law says so, and the law must be obeyed, right or wrong, till it is altered. Argument always used by Jesuits and despots, on weak consciences, and weaker brains. Argument first begotten of Satan, Father of Lies. . . .

The men that refuse obedience to such laws are the sure, the only defenders of law. If they will shed their own blood rather than sin by keeping a wicked law, they will by the same principle shed their blood rather than break a law which is righteous. In short, such men are the only true law-abiding men. For they never break a law, except when they see that to keep it would be to violate all law in its very foundation, and overturn the very government of God; while those men who clamor for blind obedience to all law—right or wrong—are striking at the throne of God. . . .

In conclusion, therefore, my application of the subject is—Disobey this law. If you have ever dreamed of obeying it, repent before God, and ask His forgiveness. I counsel no violence. I suggest no warlike measures of resistance. I incite no man to deeds of blood. I speak as the minister of the Prince of Peace. As much as lieth in you, live peaceably with all men. To the fugitive, touching the question of self-defense, I offer no advice, as none can be necessary. The right of self-defense is unquestionable here, if ever. Of the expedience of its exercise, every man must judge for himself. I leave the question of self-defense undiscussed, to the settlement of every man's own judgment, according to circumstances.

But if a fugitive claim your help on his journey, break the law and give it him. The law is broken as thoroughly by indirectly aiding his escape as directly, for both are penal. Therefore break the law, and help him on his way, directly if you can, indirectly if you must. Feed him, clothe him, harbor him, by day and by night, and conceal him from his pursuers and from the officers of the law. If you are summoned to aid in his capture, refuse to obey. If you are commanded by the officer to lay hands on the fugitive, decline to comply; rather, if possible, detain the officer, if you conveniently can, without injury to his person, until the victim is clean gone. If for these things you are accused and brought to trial, appear and defend yourself. If asked how you dared disobey the laws of this realm, answer with Bunyan's Pilgrim in Vanity Fair: tell the court that you obey Christ, not Belial. If they fine you, and imprison you, take joyfully the spoiling of your goods, wear gladly your chain, and in the last day you shall be rewarded for your fidelity to God. Do not think any true disgrace can attach to such penalties. It is the devil, and the devil's people only, who enact, enforce, or respect such penalties. If you are disgraced, it is the disgrace that Washington bore when he was called a rebel, and it is inflicted on you for the support of a cause and of principles as holy as his.

You will suffer with Wickliffe and Huss, with the Albigenses and Huguenots, with the early Christian martyrs, with the Apostles, and Jesus their head; and with that mighty army of still more ancient worthies, who were stoned, sawn asunder, and of whom the world was not worthy. With them to suffer is honor; with them to be defamed, reviled, and spit upon, is glory. With them to rise and reign eternally, will be ample reward.

THE DUTY OF DISOBEDIENCE
TO THE FUGITIVE SLAVE ACT

AN APPPEAL TO THE
LEGISLATORS OF MASSACHUSETTS*
by Maria Child

I feel there is no need of apologizing to the legislature of Massachusetts because a woman addresses them. Sir Walter Scott says: "The truth of Heaven was never committed to a tongue, however feeble, but it gave a right to that tongue to announce mercy, while it declared judgment." And in view of all that women have done, and are doing, intellectually and morally, for the advancement of the world, I presume no enlightened legislator will be disposed to deny that the "truth of Heaven" is often committed to them, and that they sometimes utter it with a degree of power that greatly influences the age in which they live.

I therefore offer no excuses on that score. But I do feel as if it required some apology to attempt to convince men of ordinary humanity and common sense that the Fugitive Slave Bill is utterly wicked, and consequently ought never to be obeyed. Yet Massachusetts consents to that law! Some shadow of justice she grants, inasmuch as her Legislature have passed what is called a Personal Liberty Bill, securing trial by jury to those claimed as slaves. Certainly it is something gained, especially for those who may get brown by working in the sunshine, to prevent our Southern masters from taking any of us, at a moment's notice, and dragging us off into perpetual bondage. It is something gained to require legal proof that a man is a slave, before he is given up to arbitrary torture and unrecompensed toil. But is that the measure of justice becoming the

---

*Excerpts from Anti-Slavery Tract No. 9, published by the American Anti-Slavery Society, Boston (1860).

character of a free Commonwealth? "Prove that the man is property, according to your laws, and I will drive him into your cattle-pen with sword and bayonet," is what Massachusetts practically says to Southern tyrants. "Show me a Bill of Sale from the Almighty!" is what she ought to say. No other proof should be considered valid in a Christian country.

One thousand five hundred years ago, Gregory, a Bishop in Asia Minor, preached a sermon in which he rebuked the sin of slaveholding. Indignantly he asked, "Who can be the possessor of human beings save God? Those men that you say belong to you, did not God create them free? Command the brute creation; that is well. Bend the beasts of the field beneath your yoke. But are your fellow-men to be bought and sold, like herds of cattle? Who can pay the value of a being created in the image of God? The whole world itself bears no proportion to the value of a soul, on which the Most High has set the seal of his likeness. This world will perish, but the soul of man is immortal. Show me, then, your titles of possession. Tell me whence you derive this strange claim. Is not your own nature the same with that of those you call your slaves? Have they not the same origin with yourselves? Are they not born to the same immortal destinies?"

Thus spake a good old Bishop, in the early years of Christianity. Since then, thousands and thousands of noble should have given their bodies to the gibbet and the stake, to help onward the slow progress of truth and freedom; a great unknown continent has been opened as a new, free starting point for the human race; printing has been invented, and the command, "Whatsoever ye would that men should do unto you, do ye even so unto them," has been sent abroad in all the languages of the earth. And here, in the noon-day light of the nineteenth century, in a nation claiming to be the freest and most enlightened on the face of the globe, a portion of the population of fifteen States have thus agreed among themselves: "Other men shall work for us, without wages, while we smoke, and drink, and gamble, and race horses, and fight. We will have their wives and daughters for concubines, and sell their children in the market with horses and pigs. If they make any objection to this arrangement, we will break them into subjection with the cow-hide and the bucking-paddle. They shall not be permitted to read or write, because that would be likely to 'produce dissatisfaction in their minds.' If they attempt to run away from us, our blood-hounds shall tear the flesh from their bones, and any man who sees them may shoot them down like mad dogs. If they succeed in getting beyond our frontier, into States where it is the custom to pay men for their work, and to protect their wives and children from outrage, we will compel the people of those States to drive them back into the jaws of our blood-hounds." . . .

Shame on my native State! Everlasting shame! Blot out the escutcheon of the brave old Commonwealth! Instead of the sword uplifted to protect liberty, let the slave-driver's whip be suspended over a blood-hound, and take for your motto, Obedience to tyrants is the highest law. . . .

If you resort to the alleged legal obligation to return fugitives, it has more plausibility, but has it in reality any firm foundation? Americans boast of making their own laws, and of amending them whenever circumstances render it necessary. How, then, can they excuse themselves, or expect the civilized world to excuse them for making, or sustaining, unjust and cruel laws? The Fugitive Slave Act has none of the attributes of law. If two highwaymen agreed between themselves to stand by each other in robbing helpless men, women and children, should we not find it hard work to "conquer our prejudices" so far as to dignify their bargain with the name of law? That is the light in which the compact between North and South presents itself to the minds of intelligent slaves, and we should view it in the same way, if we were in their position. Law was established to maintain justice between man and man; and this Act clearly maintains injustice. Law was instituted to protect the weak from the strong; this Act delivers the weak completely into the arbitrary power of the strong. "Law is a rule of conduct, prescribed by the supreme power, commanding what is right, and forbidding what is wrong." This is the commonly received definition of law, and obviously, none more correct could be substituted for it. The application of it would at once annul the Fugitive Slave Act, and abolish slavery. That Act reverses the maxim. It commands what is wrong, and forbids what is right. It commands us to trample on the weak and defenseless, to persecute the oppressed, to be accomplices in defrauding honest laborers of their wages. It forbids us to shelter the homeless, to protect abused innocents, to feed the hungry, to "hide the outcast." Let theological casuists argue as they will, Christian hearts will shrink from thinking of Jesus as surrendering a fugitive slave; or of any of His apostles, unless it be Judas. Political casuists may exercise their skill in making the worse appear the better reason, still all honest minds have an intuitive perception that no human enactment which violates God's laws is worthy of respect. . . .

There is another consideration, which ought alone to have sufficient weight with us to deter us from attempting to carry out this tyrannical enactment. All history, and all experience, show it to be an immutable law of God, that whosoever injures another, injures himself in the process. These frequent scuffles between despotism and freedom, with despotism shielded by law, cannot otherwise than demoralize our people. They unsettle the popular mind concerning eternal principles of justice. They harden the heart by familiarity with violence. They accustom people to the idea that it is right for Capital to own Labor; and thus the reverence for Liberty, which we inherited from our fathers, will gradually die out in the souls of our children. We are compelled to disobey our own consciences, and repress all our humane feelings, or else to disobey the law. It is a grievous wrong done to the people to place them between these alternatives. The inevitable result is to destroy the sanctity of law. The doctrine that "might makes right," which our rulers consent to teach the people, in order to pacify slaveholders, will come out in unexpected forms to disturb our own peace and safety. There is "even-handed justice" in the fact that men cannot aid in enslaving others, and themselves remain free; that they cannot assist in robbing others, without endangering their own security.

Moreover, there is wrong done, even to the humblest individual, when he is compelled to be ashamed of his country. When the judge passed under chains into Boston Court House, and when Anthony Burns was sent back into slavery, I wept for my native State, as a daughter weeps for the crimes of a beloved mother. It seemed to me that I would gladly have died to have saved Massachusetts from that sin and that shame. The tears of a secluded woman, who has no vote to give, may appear to you of little consequence. But assuredly it is not well with any Commonwealth, when her daughters weep over her degeneracy and disgrace.

In the name of oppressed humanity, of violated religion, of desecrated law, or tarnished honor, of our own freedom endangered, of the moral sense of our people degraded by these evil influences, I respectfully, but most urgently, entreat you to annul this infamous enactment, so far as the jurisdiction of Massachusetts extends. Our old Commonwealth has been first and foremost in many good works; let her lead in this also. And deem it not presumptuous, if I ask it likewise for my own sake. I am a humble member of the community; but I am deeply interested in the welfare and reputation of my native State, and that gives me some claim to be heard. I am growing old; and on this great question of equal rights I have toiled for years, sometimes with a heart sickened by "hope deferred." I beseech you to let me die on Free Soil! Grant me the satisfaction of saying, ere I go hence–

> "Slaves cannot breathe among us. If their lungs
> Receive our air, that moment they are free!
> They touch our country, and their shackles fall!"

If you cannot be induced to reform this great wickedness, for the sake of outraged justice and humanity, then do it for the honor of the State, for the political welfare of our own people, for the moral character of our posterity. For, as sure as there is a Righteous Ruler in the heavens, if you continue to be accomplices in violence and fraud, God will not "save the Commonwealth of Massachusetts."

FINAL STATEMENT OF COUNSEL IN ROITMAN & PALMER WOMEN'S CLINICAL GROUP, INC. v. ANN O'BRIEN, ET AL.

St. Louis County, Missouri Circuit Court
October 3, 1984

What I want to say to the Court today by way of a final argument on behalf of these defendants needs a little introduction. They have been tried for contempt of this Court, and my comments necessarily will include rather strong statements regarding judicial power, and the effects of judicial acts, judicial conscience and responsibility, where court-made law comes into direct conflict with basic moral values.

I will not mean by these statements to show disrespect for the court, or particularly this Court; on the contrary, my acquaintance with Your Honor over several years of practice has resulted in my having the highest regard for this Court in particular.

But as a lawyer, I have taken an oath, the last paragraph of which says "that I will never reject, from any consideration personal to myself, the cause of the defenseless or oppressed . . . so help me God." Like every member of the Bar, I have a responsibility to be faithful to that oath, as well as to my conscience.

I speak of this now for, after all, each of these defendants is here on these contempt charges because he or she has responded to one of the highest calls of conscience: to help the oppressed, to intervene for the helpless, to become a voice for the one who has no voice: the unborn child.

So I will not speak primarily for the rights of these defendants, though their rights are in jeopardy at this hour. They want me to speak for the rights of another person, on whose behalf they have acted. It is this person who motivated these defendants to do what they did. Their focus was on that little human being. For that reason, I would like the Court to look at the day of one of these demonstrations at the abortion clinic through the eyes of that little one.

I will speak for this little one in the first person because my clients' consciences and Bibles require them to speak for this one who cannot yet speak for himself, and I in turn must speak for my clients.

"I know why I am brought here today—because I was here a few days ago and I heard what would happen today. My mother set an appointment to have me killed. I can't believe it. But as we get out of the car, I look around and I am encouraged because I see some people walking back and forth carrying signs. These signs ask my mother to change her mind. The people carrying them are the only friendly faces I've ever seen.

"But now we are going on past these people who are 'peacefully picketing,' and I realize that my mother has not changed her mind. Those picketers were friendly; they may help someone like me, sometime, somewhere, but it doesn't look like they can help me—not today.

"Now we are in the atrium, and I know we're getting closer. There are more people in here. Some are singing; some are praying. Now someone stops my mother and warns her not to kill me! But she goes on by. We are nearing the door to the clinic. I know what's beyond that door.

"We are stopped for a minute, and I hear someone talking about Washington, and about the elections in November. November 6, they say—and they say this problem will maybe be taken care of after that. But this is September 14, and my 'problem' is today. Can't somebody think about just me for a minute?

"Now we are right at the door, but my mother is not going in yet. A man is standing in her way. He will not move. He seems determined. He is the first person I've met who personally cares about just me.

"I think my mother may turn back now. I hope that man does not leave the doorway until she does."

Now the question before the Court today is this: can any rule of law, should any rule of law, remove that man from that doorway?

Or, if such a rule is established by injunction or otherwise, should it, can it be obeyed? I believe this Court is satisfied that the defendants' motives here were honorable—to save lives—but that the action they took, no matter how well motivated, was in fact contemptuous, because it violated a court order. That was the actual result, no matter the motives.

But the same analysis can be made of the Court's order. Your Honor entered it for two reasons: to prevent economic loss to the plaintiff, and to prevent disorderliness at the clinic. This is referred to as "domestic tranquility"—keeping the peace.

So the Court's order was well-motivated; its objectives were proper. But its actual effect is disastrous. It removes that man from the door. It clears the path so that no one can block the death of this particular unborn child. And while its objectives were good, was it not issued primarily to protect the income of these doctors—a virtually insignificant value compared to the life of a child?

If the Court were to convict the defendants in this case, the doctors' economic well-being would be placed on at least as high a plane as innocent human life. Bare rule of law, and (in this case) the responsibility of the Christian citizen to obey the civil magistrate, would be imposed—even when that law forbids the citizen to intervene in the death of the helpless.

I know that this Court has a strong interest in seeing that its orders are obeyed. You must uphold the majesty of the court, and the majesty of the law. But that majesty can never be upheld through the advancement or protection of evil laws.

The witnesses have stated that pregnant women actually have been turned away from this clinic during September. They have changed their minds; they have called the adoption agency because of the defendants' actions here.

What it comes down to is this: this Court, or any trial court for that matter, can almost unwittingly be used by the powers that be as the enforcement arm for evil, reprehensible, immoral law. This Court, perhaps, is somewhat unique. You have already expressed the Court's position, on the record, that the *Roe v. Wade* decision was wrong, morally wrong, because Your Honor has accepted it as a fact that a human being begins his life at conception.

If it were not for *Roe v. Wade*, this Court would be the forum today for the criminal prosecution of doctors who kill, the way it used to be before 1973. I am convinced Your Honor believes as a matter of conscience that would be the right course of action for this Court, and for this country. It would be an amazing and awful thing if *Roe v. Wade*, or any decision, could require you to impose criminal sanctions against those who intervene in the death of the helpless, in favor of those who profit from killing them.

Such a result, Your Honor, should be unthinkable. Judicial conscience does not allow it.

Yesterday Your Honor asked the lawyers to outline what Scriptural motivation or rationale these defendants claim as their basis for violating the Court's order. They have testified about that, but in closing I would include here just one such Scriptural mandate—one which not only explains their actions but also grips the consciences of the rest of us. It is Proverbs 24, verses 11 and 12:

> Rescue those being led away to death;
>   hold back those staggering towards slaughter.
> If you say, "But we knew nothing about this,"
>   does not he who weighs the heart perceive it?
> Does not he who guards your life know it?
> Will he not repay each person according to
>   what he has done?

PROCLAMATION 5761 OF JANUARY 14, 1988

*NATIONAL SANCTITY OF HUMAN LIFE DAY, 1988**

By the President of the United States of America

A PROCLAMATION

America has given a great gift to the world, a gift that drew upon the accumulated wisdom derived from centuries of experiments in self-government, a gift that has irrevocably changed humanity's future. Our gift is twofold: the declaration, as a cardinal principle of all just law, of the God-given, unalienable rights possessed by every human being; and the example of our determination to secure those rights and to defend them against every challenge through the generations. Our declaration and defense of our rights have made us and kept us free and have sent a tide of hope and inspiration around the globe.

One of those unalienable rights, as the Declaration of Independence affirms so eloquently, is the right to life. In the 15 years since the Supreme Court's decision in *Roe v. Wade*, however, America's unborn have been denied their right to life. Among the tragic and unspeakable results in the past decade and a half have been the loss of life of 22 million infants before birth; the pressure and anguish of countless women and girls who are driven to abortion; and a cheapening of our respect for the human person and the sanctity of human life.

We are told that we may not interfere with abortion. We are told that we may not "impose our morality" on those who wish to allow or participate in the taking of the life of infants before birth; yet no one calls it "imposing morality" to prohibit the taking of life after people are born. We are told as well that there exists a "right"

---

*Published in the *Federal Register*, Vol. 53, No. 11, Tuesday, January 19, 1988.

to end the lives of unborn children; yet no one can explain how such a right can exist in stark contradiction of each person's fundamental right to life.

That right to life belongs equally to babies in the womb, babies born handicapped, and the elderly or infirm. That we have killed the unborn for 15 years does not nullify this right, nor could any number of killings ever do so. The unalienable right to life is found not only in the Declaration of Independence but also in the Constitution that every President is sworn to preserve, protect, and defend. Both the Fifth and Fourteenth Admendments guarantee that no person shall be deprived of life without due process of law.

All medical and scientific evidence increasingly affirms that children before birth share all the basic attributes of human personality—that they in fact are persons. Modern medicine treats unborn children as patients. Yet, as the Supreme Court itself has noted, the decision in *Roe v. Wade* rested upon an earlier state of medical technology. The law of the land in 1988 should recognize all of the medical evidence.

Our Nation cannot continue down the path of abortion, so radically at odds with our history, our heritage, and our concepts of justice. This sacred legacy, and the well-being and the future of our country, demand that protection of the innocents must be guaranteed and that the personhood of the unborn be declared and defended throughout our land. In legislation introduced at my request in the First Session of the 100th Congress, I have asked the Legislative branch to declare the "humanity of the unborn child and the compelling interest of the several states to protect the life of each person before birth." This duty to declare on so fundamental a matter falls to the Executive as well. By this Proclamation I hereby do so.

NOW, THEREFORE, I, RONALD REAGAN, President of the United States of America, by virtue of the authority vested in me by the Constitution and laws of the United States, do hereby proclaim and declare the unalienable personhood of every American, from the moment of conception until natural death, and I do proclaim, ordain, and declare that I will take care that the Constitution and laws of the United States are faithfully executed for the protection of America's unborn children. Upon this act, sincerely believed to be an act of justice, warranted by the Constitution, I invoke the considerate judgment of mankind and the gracious favor of Almighty God. I also proclaim Sunday, January 17, 1988, as National Sanctity of Human Life Day. I call upon the citizens of this blessed land to gather on that day in their homes and places of worship to give thanks for the gift of life they enjoy and to reaffirm their commitment to the dignity of every human being and the sanctity of every human life.

IN WITNESS WHEREOF, I have hereunto set my hand this 14th day of January, in the year of our Lord nineteen hundred and eighty-eight, and of the Independence of the United States of America the two hundred and twelfth.

Signed,
Ronald Reagan

NOTES

PREFACE

1. Just eight years before *Roe v. Wade*, the Supreme Court had struck down a Connecticut law that prohibited the use of certain birth control devices. That case, *Griswold v. Connecticut*, 381 U.S. 479 (1965), based its reasoning on the "right to privacy"—admittedly an implied, not a specified, right—in the U.S. Constitution. The *Griswold* case was cited in *Roe v. Wade* as precedent.
2. *The Wall Street Journal*, December 8, 1988, "Anti-Abortion Movement's Anti-Establishment Face."
3. Randall A. Terry, *Operation Rescue* (Springdale, PA: Whitaker House, 1988), p. 18.
4. Many pro-life activists resist the use of the terms "doctors" to refer to abortionists and "clinics" to refer to their offices, because they believe that such professional terms give unmerited status and respect to those involved in the business of killing babies. The terms "abortionists," "murderers," or "baby-killers" are used for the abortionist doctors, and terms like "abortuary" are used for abortion clinics. I prefer to continue to use the words "clinics" and "doctors" because in fact abortionists and their businesses have full professional status within the American medical community. It is that medical community of professionals that has led the way in promoting abortion rights, and it is important for us and for the public continually to be reminded of the fact that it is *licensed doctors* who are in the abortion business today. The full weight of that embarrassment should be brought to bear on the medical community, and we lift some of that weight if we, in our terminology, separate abortionists from the medical community.

CHAPTER ONE: The Weight of the Abortion Issue

1. *Roe v. Wade*, 410 U.S. 113 (1973).
2. Report of the Ad Interim Committee on Abortion, adopted by the Sixth General Assembly of the Presbyterian Church in America, Grand Rapids, Michigan, June 19-23, 1978, p. 11.
3. An abortion as envisioned by *Roe v. Wade* always involves two people because of the necessary involvement of the woman's doctor. The recent development and marketing of drugs producing "spontaneous"

abortions may ultimately mean that a woman could self-induce an abortion without the participation of a doctor. But so far such drugs, like RU 486, which was approved by the French government in September 1988, are prescription drugs, and would at least require the "participation" of a doctor in the decision-making process, if not in the procedure itself.

4. The 1973 Supreme Court made it clear that an abortion could be obtained only after the pregnant woman *consulted* with her physician: "This means, on the other hand, that, for the period of pregnancy prior to this 'compelling' point, the attending physician, in consultation with his patient, is free to determine, without regulation by the State, that, in his medical judgment, the patient's pregnancy should be terminated. If that decision is reached, the judgment may be effectuated by an abortion free of interference by the State." *Roe v. Wade*, 410 U.S. 113, 163.

5. The American Law Institute, *Model Penal Code* §§210.1 and 210.2 (Philadelphia, 1985). This model code, in another section, defines "human being" as a person who has been born and is alive, thus technically excluding the killing of the unborn from the definition of murder (§210.0). Note also that both the *Model Penal Code* and Old Testament law legitimize the intentional taking of human life under certain circumstances, such as in self-defense and capital punishment.

6. *Dred Scott v. Sandford* 60 U.S. (19 How.) 393 (1857).

7. *Roe v. Wade*, 410 U.S. 113, 153.

8. *Thornburgh v. American College of Obstetricians and Gynecologists, et al.,* 106 S.Ct. 2169 (1986) (Burger, J., dissenting).

9. *The St. Louis Post-Dispatch*, June 7, 1988, p. 2B.

10. *Roe v. Wade*, 410 U.S. 113, 158.

11. *Ibid.*, p. 153.

12. *Akron v. Akron Center for Reproductive Health*, 462 U.S. 416 (1983).

13. W. H. Siebert, *The Underground Railroad* (Columbus, OH: Ohio State University Press, 1898), p. 271.

14.   *Statutes at Large*, IX, pp. 462-465, 5 (1850).

15. Monica M. Migliorino, "Report from Rats' Alley: Down and Out with the Unborn in Chicago and Milwaukee," *Fidelity* Magazine (July-August 1987), p. 39.

16. Genesis 2:23a.

CHAPTER TWO: *The Demand for Moral Integrity*

1. Heinz Ullstein's memoirs, *Spielplatz meines lebens* (Munich, 1961), pp. 338-340. This passage was translated in *Peace News* (March 19, 1965) in an article by Theodor Ebert, "Effects of Repression by the Invader," and appears also in *The Politics of Nonviolent Action*, by Gene Sharp (Boston: Porter Sargent, 1973), pp. 89, 90.

2. Matthew 5:14, 15.
3. Verse 16.
4. John 3:19, 20.
5. Henry David Thoreau, "On the Duty of Civil Disobedience," The New English Library Limited, London, 1960, p. 226.

CHAPTER THREE: *Standing in the Way*

1. "True Believer," by Peter Carlson, *The Washington Post Magazine* (March 20, 1988), pp. 24-30.
2. Actually it is the Declaration of Independence that states that men "are endowed by their Creator with certain unalienable Rights. . . ." But those values and principles are carried forward throughout the Constitution.
3. *Roitman and Palmer Women's Clinical Group, Inc., a Corp., v. Ann O'Brien, et al.,* in the Circuit Court of the County of St. Louis, State of Missouri, Case No. 494962, before the Hon. Robert Lee Campbell, Judge, transcript of proceedings, November 26, 1984.
4. *Pensacola News Journal*, September 25, 1986, p. 18A.
5. Presentence Investigation, re: Joan Andrews, prepared by Richard G. Sharpless and Robert D. Mann of the Florida Department of Corrections, September 17, 1986.
6. *State of Florida v. Joan Elizabeth Andrews,* in the Circuit Court in and for Escambia County, Florida, Case No. 86-1663-CFA5, Order of William H. Anderson, Circuit Judge, September 25, 1986.

CHAPTER FOUR: *What Scripture Says*

1. Actions which involve violence, such as the bombing of an abortion clinic or setting fire to a clinic, always involve substantial risk to innocent lives. The issue of potential violence in the pro-life activist movement is discussed more fully in Chapter Twelve of this book, "Objection 5."
2. Much of the material for this chapter is from a paper prepared by the author and The Rev. Linward Crowe, which was submitted to, revised, and approved by the Church-State Subcommittee of the Committee on Administration of the Presbyterian Church in America, an evangelical Presbyterian denomination. The paper is entitled "Propriety of the Christian's Non-violent Disobedience to the Civil Magistrate in the Abortion Controversy," and was approved by the Church-State Subcommittee on March 7, 1986. It was later approved by the Committee on Administration, and in June 1987 was received as information by the General Assembly of the Presbyterian Church in America meeting in Grand Rapids, Michigan.

3. Romans 13:1-5.
CD 4. See also Titus 3:1 and 1 Timothy 2:1, 2.
5. Ephesians 5:22—6:9.
6. Luke 20:20-26 and Romans 13:6, 7.
7. John 19:10, 11.
8. Exodus 1:15-22. ↵
CD 9. Hebrews 11:23.
10. Joshua 2.✔
CD11. Hebrews 11:31.
CD 12. Joshua 6:17b, 25.
13. 1 Kings 18:1-15.✔
14. Jeremiah 27:12-15.
15. Jeremiah 34:1-7.
16. Jeremiah 52:10, 11.
17. Daniel 3:16-18. ↵
18. 2 Peter 3:7.
19. 2 Peter 3:14.
20. Westminster Shorter Catechism, Question 14.
21. 1 John 3:4.
22. James 4:17.
23. Acts 4:18, 19.✔
24. Acts 5:18.
25. Acts 5:29.
26. Luke 13:10-14.
27. Luke 13:15-17.
28. John Calvin, *Institutes of the Christian Religion*, Book IV, Chapter 20, Section 32 (emphasis supplied).

CHAPTER FIVE: Christian Duty and Abortion

1. Leviticus 19:18; Matthew 22:39.
2. Proverbs 24:11, 12.
3. Luke 10:25-27; Deuteronomy 6:5; Leviticus 19:18.
4. Luke 10:30-35.
5. Luke 10:36, 37.
6. Matthew 22:37-40.
7. Matthew 7:12.
8. Mark 12:40; Isaiah 1:16-20; Exodus 22:22; Micah 6:8; 1 Thessalonians 5:5, 22; James 1:27.
9. 1 Timothy 2:1, 2; Romans 13.
10. Romans 13:10.
11. John Calvin, *Institutes of the Christian Religion*, Book IV, Chapter 20, Section 32.
12. *Roe v. Wade*, 410 U.S. 113,153 (1973).
13. Dante's *Inferno*, Third Canto.

CHAPTER SIX: *Historical Precedent: The Underground Railroad*

1. Marion Gleason McDougall, *Fugitive Slaves [1619-1865]* (Boston, 1891), republished by Bergman Publishers (New York: Ayer, 1967), pp.105, 106. This first Fugitive Slave Law of 1793 was actually entitled, "An Act respecting fugitives from justice and persons escaping from the service of their masters," clustering slaves fleeing from bondage with criminals or criminal suspects fleeing from prosecution.
2. *Ibid.*, pp. 112, 115.
3. W. H. Siebert, *The Underground Railroad* (Columbus, OH: Ohio State University Press, 1898), p. 111.
4. Levi Coffin, *Reminiscences of Levi Coffin*, third edition (Cincinnati, 1898), republished by Arno Press and the *New York Times* (New York, 1968), pp.19, 20.
5. Siebert, p. 111.
6. *Ibid.*, p. 110.
7. *Ibid.*, p. 111.
8. *Ibid.*, pp. 96, 97.
9. McDougall, pp. 49, 59, 60; Siebert, p. 109.
10. Excerpts of Charles Beecher's sermon "The Duty of Disobedience to Wicked Laws," which he delivered in 1851, are included in this book as Appendix A. Another powerful statement on the subject was made by Maria Child before the legislature of Massachusetts, excerpts of which are set forth in Appendix B, entitled "The Duty of Disobedience to the Fugitive Slave Act."
11. Siebert, pp. 243, 244.
12. Abraham Lincoln, "The 'Lost' Speech" at Bloomington, 1856.
13. Coffin, pp. 192, 193.
14. *Ibid.*, p. 88.
15. J. C. Willke, M.D., *Abortion and Slavery: History Repeats* (Cincinnati: Hayes, 1984).
16. Lewis E. Lehrman, "The Right to Life and the Restoration of the American Republic," *National Review* (August 29, 1986), p. 26.
17. This Proclamation is set forth in full in Appendix D.

CHAPTER SEVEN: *Historical Precedent: Le Chambon*

1. Michael R. Marrus and Robert O. Paxton, *Vichy France and the Jews* (New York: Schocken, 1981), p. 96.
2. *Ibid.*, p. 206.
3. Jeanne Merle d'Aubigné and Violette Mouchon, *God's Underground* (St. Louis, 1970).
4. *Ibid.*, pp. 113ff.; Philip P. Hallie, *Lest Innocent Blood Be Shed* (New York: Harper & Row, 1979).
5. Hallie, p. 120.
6. *Ibid.*, p. 108.

7. *Ibid.*, p. 44.

8. André Trocmé, "The Law Itself Was a Lie!" (*Fellowship*   magazine, January 1955), pp. 4-9.

9. Romans 13:9b, 10.

10. Hallie, pp. 110, 111.

11. *Ibid.*, p. 69.

12. 1 Peter 2:17b.

13. Hallie, p. 143.

CHAPTER EIGHT: *Activism, Abortion, and Anarchy*

1. Daniel B. Stevick, *Civil Disobedience and the Christian* (New York, 1969), p. 15.

2. F. Kefa Sempangi, *A Distant Grief* (Glendale, CA: Regal, 1979), pp. 100, 101.

3. Missouri Revised Statutes, §563.026(1). However, the Missouri Court of Appeals, Eastern District, has ruled that this defense is not available in cases involving trespass at an abortion clinic, reasoning that the legislature, in allowing such a defense to be raised, did not mean to allow someone to intervene to prevent public or private injury, where the activity which produces the injury perceived by the trespasser is legal, or constitutionally protected, as is a woman's right to have an abortion under *Roe v. Wade*.

4. It has previously been noted, in Chapter Seven, that this argument is supported in Scripture. Daniel, for example, disobeyed King Darius as to the particular evil law which forbade his prayers. Daniel did not obey the law until things got worse, nor did he seek the overthrow of the government. To the contrary, he disobeyed the law and gave his allegiance to King Darius as he was lifted from the lions' den.

5. 839 F.2d 1941 (9th Cir. 1988).

6. 18 U.S.C. § 1111.

7. *U. S. v. Spencer*, at 1343 (emphasis supplied).

8. *Thornburgh v. American College of Obstetricians and Gynecologists* , *et al..*, 106 S.Ct. 2169 (1986) (Burger, J., dissenting).

9. Lewis E. Lehrman, "The Right to Life and the Restoration of the American Republic," *National Review* (August 29, 1986), p. 26.

CHAPTER NINE: *Solidarity with the Unborn*

1. *Webster's Third New International Dictionary*.

2. Joan Andrews, "A Case for Pro-Se Vulnerability in Court," Escambia County Jail, Pensacola, Florida, July 15, 1986.

3. Ephesians 2:12.

4. Hebrews 2:17.

5. Hebrews 5:7.

6. Matthew 7:24-27.
7. Ezekiel 33:30-33.
8. Harold O. J. Brown, "The Abortion Issue and the Integrity of the Church," *The Presbyterian Communique*, September-October 1979.
9. Henry David Thoreau, "On the Duty of Civil Disobedience," The New English Library Limited, London, 1960, p. 226.
10. Paul McClelland Angle, *The Lincoln Reader* (New Brunswick, NJ: Rutgers University Press, 1947), pp. 492, 493.

CHAPTER TEN: Commitment to Action

1. The author asked a court to consider this question in a trial in St. Louis County in October 1984, by focusing on the trip into the abortion clinic from the viewpoint of the unborn child. That statement is set forth in full in Appendix C.
2. Joseph Scheidler, *Closed: 99 Ways To Stop Abortion* (Westchester, IL: Crossway Books, 1985).
3. Ezekiel 22:29-31.
4. Ephesians 6:12.
5. J. I. Packer, *Knowing God* (Downers Grove, IL: InterVarsity Press, 1973), pp. 245, 246.

CHAPTER ELEVEN: The Ethical Mandate and Grace

1. Mark 12:29-31.
2. Matthew 5:21-30.
3. James 1:27.
4. John Murray, *Principles of Conduct* (Grand Rapids, MI: Eerdmans, 1957), p. 202.
5. David C. Jones, "Ethics Catechism" (St. Louis, 1988). Dr. Jones, professor of systematic theology at Covenant Theological Seminary, has drafted a short outline on the subject of Christian ethics, in catechetical form. Question 1 is: What is the goal of life? Answer: God. Question 2 is: How can a person become willing at heart to seek this goal? Answer: By grace. Jones continues: "More precisely, by the work of the Holy Spirit who in regeneration creates a disposition of faith, hope and love (the evangelical virtues). The *impelling motive* of the Christian life is *love for God* with all one's heart and mind and soul and strength, and consequently love for one's neighbor as oneself. Christian love is the reverent, thankful, obedient response of those who have experienced the love of God in Christ."
6. Herman Ridderbos, *Paul: An Outline of His Theology* (Grand Rapids, MI: Eerdmans, 1975), p. 228.
7. Psalm 37:5, 6.
8. Hebrews 11:32-35a.

9. Romans 2:12-16.
10. 1 Kings 17:7-24.
11. Colossians 1:16, 17.
12. John 19:11.
13. 2 Peter 2:7, 8.
14. 1 Timothy 2:1-4.
15. Hebrews 13:3.
16. Psalm 90:17.

CHAPTER TWELVE: *Objections Considered*

1. 2 Corinthians 10:5b.
2. Isaiah 58:6, 7.
3. Randall A. Terry, *Operation Rescue* (Springdale, PA: Whitaker House, 1988), pp. 228, 229.
4. Paul B. Fowler, *Abortion: Toward an Evangelical Consensus* (Portland, OR: Multnomah, 1987), p. 192.
5. Romans 13:4b.
6. Martin Luther King, Jr., *Why We Can't Wait* (New York: New American Library, 1964), and *The Trumpet of Conscience* (New York, 1968).

INDEX